Calphalon Cooks Weekends

By the Culinary Staff at Calphalon

Developmental Editor
Linda J. Selden

Art Directors
Vasken Guiragossian and
Pamela Hoch

Research & Text
Sandra Cameron and
Cynthia Scheer

Copy Editor
Rebecca LaBrum

Photography
Chris Shorten

Food Stylist
Susan Massey

Food Stylist Assistant
Danielle Di Salvo

Production Coordinator
Patricia S. Williams

Props
Sur la Table, San Francisco

Sunset Books Inc.

Editorial Director
Bob Doyle

First Edition. June 1997.
Copyright © 1997 Calphalon Corporation,
Toledo, Ohio 43697-0583. All rights reserved,
including the right of
reproduction in whole or part in any form.
ISBN 0-376-00168-2
Library of Congress Catalog Card Number:
97-60559.
Printed in the United States.

A Word About Our Nutritional Data

For our recipes, we provide a nutritional analysis stating calorie count; grams of total fat and saturated fat; milligrams of cholesterol and sodium; grams of carbohydrates, fiber, and protein; and milligrams of calcium and iron. Generally, the analysis applies to a single serving, based on the number of servings given for each recipe and the amount of each ingredient. If a range is given for the number of servings and/or the amount of an ingredient, the analysis is based on the average of the figures given.

The nutritional analysis does not include optional ingredients or those for which no specific amount is stated. If an ingredient is listed with a substitution, the information was calculated using the first choice.

Preparation and cooking times are provided for each recipe. Keep in mind that these times are approximate and will vary depending on your expertise in the kitchen and on the cooking equipment you use.

CONTENTS

Meals for Leisurely Weekends

Good cooks look forward to the weekends with particular anticipation. Those two days offer the luxury of extra time—time to cook in ways that the rush of a weeknight doesn't allow. Perhaps you'll make fried chicken as grandmother did, or bake a cake or pie from scratch. Weekends are also a time to enjoy meals away from home, taking favorite dishes to the beach or even cooking them in the rustic kitchen of a cabin in the woods. For all these pleasurable occasions, turn to Calphalon cookware and this book. And because even the most committed cooks don't want to spend all their precious weekend hours in the kitchen, these recipes include preparation and cooking times to guide your selections. Menus are provided, but feel free to embellish or adapt them as you please.

COOKING WITH CALPHALON

Quality and versatility are two good reasons to choose durable Calphalon *Hard-Anodized Cookware* for every kind of weekend cooking. The handsome pans are made from heavy-gauge aluminum, one of the most conductive of all metals used for cookware.

First spun or drawn into one of many classic shapes and sizes, the pans then undergo the electrochemical process of hard-anodization—giving them a hard, non-porous surface that's an integral part of each pan, not just a surface coating. That means you can use a metal spatula or tongs for turning foods and a wire whisk to stir sauces when you cook in Calphalon. These pans are matchless for a wide variety of cooking techniques: sautéing, stir-frying, braising, roasting, and baking.

Calphalon pans heat quickly and evenly. Because heat is distributed so uniformly over the pans' smooth surface, food seldom sticks during cooking. What's more, meats, poultry, and fish brown beautifully in a Calphalon sauté pan or omelette pan, enabling you to finish off a quick sautéed dish such as Chicken Valencia (page 75) with a stylish sauce that takes advantage of the flavorful pan drippings.

Some styles of Calphalon pans have long handles of sturdy nickel-chrome plated cast iron, while others have loop handles of nickel-chrome plated steel. Such pans are appropriate for cooking on the range top as well as for baking or broiling—so you can start a dish on top of the range, then complete it in the oven.

CARING FOR YOUR CALPHALON

The most important step in keeping your Calphalon cookware in top-notch condition is washing it thoroughly (by hand, not in the dishwasher) in hot, sudsy water after each use. If any cooking residue remains, use a Scotch-Brite® pad to remove it, with a household cleanser such as Ajax® or Comet® if necessary. Dormond, a cleanser made specifically for Calphalon, can also be used; look for it in stores where Calphalon is sold.

Keep your Calphalon cookware in shape by taking care not to hit the rim with the sharp handle of a spoon or other utensil. And do your cutting and chopping before you place food in the pan; using a sharp knife in the pan itself can mar the surface.

After you finish cooking, let the pan cool completely; then, if necessary, pour water into it to loosen cooked-on food. Never immerse a warm pan in cold water, since it may become warped.

Many Calphalon pans—the oval au gratin pan and the paella pan in particular—are so handsome that they can go directly from kitchen to table. After the meal is over, promptly transfer any leftovers to another container, so the food can be cooled quickly and then covered airtight for storage in the refrigerator.

OTHER KINDS OF CALPHALON COOKWARE

In addition to Hard-Anodized cookware, Calphalon makes other types of cookware suited to a variety of cooking styles. *Commercial Nonstick* and *Professional Nonstick*, both made with the same materials and in the same way as Calphalon Hard-Anodized cookware, are especially useful for low-fat cooking. Commercial Nonstick pans have a hard-anodized exterior, cast stainless steel handles that stay cool during cooking, and stainless steel or tempered glass lids. Professional Nonstick pans have tempered glass lids and a coated exterior for easy cleaning. Both sorts of pans have a durable nonstick interior that wipes clean with a sponge. Pans as well as lids can be used in the oven up to a temperature of 450°F (230°C), but they should not go under the broiler. Use nylon, plastic, or wooden utensils to help preserve the nonstick surface, and wash the pans by hand.

For those who prefer to cook in stainless steel, there's *Commercial Tri-Ply Stainless*. This cookware has an inner core of aluminum surrounded by two layers of stainless steel. The exterior surface is polished, the interior is satin-finished, and the pan rim is slightly flared to make pouring easy. Pan lids are made of tempered glass. These pans are oven and broiler safe, but the lids should not be used under the broiler or in an oven that is hotter than 450°F (230°C).

Commercial Stainless can be washed in the dishwasher, but you'll keep it spot-free and shinier if you wash it by hand. To remove any stuck-on food, nonabrasive cleansers such as Bon Ami®, Soft Scrub®, and Bar Keepers Friend® are recommended.

For home baking, there's sturdy *Professional Nonstick Bakeware*: standard-size cookie sheets, loaf pans, muffin pans, and round, square, and rectangular cake pans. All are made from heavy-gauge aluminum or aluminized steel, following the construction techniques used for commercial bakeware.

Professional Nonstick Bakeware has a triple-coated nonstick coating inside and a medium-gray color coating outside, allowing it to absorb and reflect heat efficiently for good texture and browning—for everything from a quick batch of Carrot Corn Muffins (page 50) to traditional cut-out Orange Butter Cookies (page 25). To cut and remove servings from these pans, use a coated or nylon spatula, since repeated use of metal utensils will damage the surface. After using a pan, remove any food residue with a sponge or soft cloth and hot, sudsy water. Baked-on stains on a pan's exterior can be removed with Bon Ami or Soft Scrub and a soft nylon cleaning pad.

When you equip the kitchen of your getaway home for weekend and vacation cooking, consider building it around Calphalon *Pots & Pans*. Light and easy to handle, this moderate-priced cookware features durable nonstick surfaces, heat-resistant composition handles, and domed stainless steel covers. Made of highly conductive aluminum, Pots & Pans heat quickly and are perfect for every kind of cooking, from simmering to sautéing and stir-frying.

Fall Yard Cleaning

The anticipation of this homey dinner will keep everyone going during a hard day's work in a chilly autumn garden. Sip hot, spicy crimson cider while a luscious chicken stew bubbles away beneath a blanket of herb-flecked dumplings.

Pea & Roasted Pecan Slaw

Chicken with Herb Dumplings

Green Beans with Sautéed Red Peppers

Apple-Cheese Crumble

Mulled Cranberry Cider   Coffee

A creamy, curry-accented dressing brings together shredded cabbage, green peas, and roasted pecans in this favorite salad. If you don't want to oven-roast the nuts, toast them in an omelette pan or sauté pan over medium-high heat, stirring them lightly until they're fragrant.

Pea & Roasted Pecan Slaw

²/₃ cup (85 g) pecan halves

1½ cups (230 g) frozen tiny peas, thawed

2 green onions, thinly sliced

2 cups (200 g) lightly packed finely shredded green cabbage

3 tablespoons (45 ml) reduced-calorie mayonnaise

2 tablespoons (30 ml) reduced-fat sour cream

2 teaspoons white wine vinegar

1 teaspoon Dijon mustard

¼ teaspoon curry powder

Romaine lettuce leaves, rinsed and crisped

Salt

Spread pecans in a shallow baking pan. Bake in a 350°F (175°C) oven until toasted (8 to 10 minutes). Set aside to cool.

Meanwhile, in a large bowl, combine peas, onions, and cabbage; mix lightly. In a small bowl, combine mayonnaise, sour cream, vinegar, mustard, and curry powder; stir until blended. (At this point, you may cover pecans and let stand at room temperature for up to 24 hours, and cover and refrigerate cabbage mixture and dressing separately for up to 24 hours.)

Just before serving, arrange lettuce leaves on a platter or in a shallow bowl. Add dressing to cabbage mixture; mix lightly. Stir in half the pecans. Season to taste with salt. Spoon salad onto lettuce-lined platter and sprinkle with remaining pecans.

Makes 4 servings

Prep: *About 15 minutes*
Cook: *8 to 10 minutes*

Per serving: *240 calories, 19 g total fat, 2 g saturated fat, 6 mg cholesterol, 177 mg sodium, 15 g carbohydrates, 6 g fiber, 6 g protein, 51 mg calcium, 2 mg iron*

Cooking tips: *Prepare romaine lettuce and other leafy greens for salad by rinsing well in cold water. Then shake off excess water and spread the lettuce on a clean kitchen towel, blotting lightly to dry well. Wrap the greens loosely in paper towels, enclose them in a plastic bag, and refrigerate for at least 30 minutes to crisp. Romaine and iceberg lettuce can be kept in the refrigerator for up to 5 days.*

Tender-crisp whole green beans mingle with garlic-sautéed red bell pepper strips and a tangle of lemon zest. The colorful bell pepper mixture can also be used to accent other steamed green vegetables, such as Brussels sprouts or broccoli.

Green Beans with Sautéed Red Peppers

12 ounces (340 g) green beans, ends trimmed

1 tablespoon (15 ml) olive oil

1½ teaspoons butter or margarine

1 small red bell pepper (about 5 oz./140 g), seeded and cut into matchstick strips

2 small cloves garlic, finely minced

Grated zest of 1 lemon

Salt and freshly ground pepper

In a 3½- or 4½-quart sauce pan fitted with a 3-quart pasta insert, bring 2 quarts (1.9 liters) water to a boil over high heat. Add beans and cook until just tender to bite (5 to 7 minutes). Remove pasta insert from cooking water and rinse beans with cold water until cool; then drain again. (At this point, you may cover beans and refrigerate for up to 24 hours.)

Preheat a 2- or 3-quart sauté pan or 10- or 12-inch omelette pan over medium-high heat until rim of pan is hot-to-the-touch. Add oil and butter and wait for about 1 more minute. Add bell pepper and garlic; cook, stirring often, until pepper is soft and garlic begins to brown (3 to 5 minutes). Reduce heat to medium, then mix in beans and lemon zest; continue to cook, stirring gently, until beans are heated through (about 3 more minutes). Season to taste with salt and pepper.

Makes 4 servings

Prep: *About 15 minutes*
Cook: *About 15 minutes*

Per serving: *76 calories, 5 g total fat, 1 g saturated fat, 4 mg cholesterol, 20 mg sodium, 8 g carbohydrates, 2 g fiber, 2 g protein, 34 mg calcium, 1 mg iron*

Cooking tips: *If you choose, you can prepare the beans for this colorful dish up to a day before serving. Cook them ahead, using the convenient Calphalon pasta insert; then rinse them with cold water, drain well, cover, and refrigerate.*

Here's a dish so good it never goes out of style. To keep the dumplings light and fluffy, cook them without peeking until it's time to check for doneness.

Chicken with Herb Dumplings

2½ to 3 pounds (1.15 to 1.35 kg) chicken pieces, such as breast halves, thighs, and/or drumsticks, skinned if desired

1½ tablespoons (23 ml) vegetable oil

1 large onion (about 8 oz./230 g), thinly sliced

6 ounces (170 g) large mushrooms, cut into quarters

4 medium-size carrots (about 8 oz./230 g total), cut into slanting 1½-inch (3.5-cm) slices

1 teaspoon dried sage

3 cups (710 ml) fat-free reduced-sodium chicken broth

¼ cup (60 ml) dry white wine

Herb Dumplings (recipe follows)

Salt and freshly ground pepper

Chopped parsley

Rinse chicken and pat dry. Preheat a 5-quart saucier pan over medium-high heat until rim of pan is hot-to-the-touch. Add oil and wait for about 1 more minute. Add chicken, about half at a time; cook, turning as needed, until browned on all sides. As chicken is browned, remove it from pan and set aside. Pour off all but about 1 tablespoon of the drippings.

Reduce heat to medium. Add onion and mushrooms to pan and cook, stirring often, until lightly browned (3 to 5 minutes). Mix in carrots and sage; then arrange chicken on top of vegetables. Pour in broth and wine. Bring mixture to a boil; then reduce heat to low, cover, and simmer for 20 minutes. Meanwhile, prepare Herb Dumplings.

Skim and discard fat from chicken mixture. Season to taste with salt and pepper. Drop dumpling dough over chicken in 8 equal portions, spacing slightly apart. Cover and continue to cook until dumplings are firm to the touch and a wooden pick inserted in center comes out clean (20 to 25 minutes). Sprinkle with parsley. Serve dumplings and chicken in wide, shallow bowls, with sauce and vegetables spooned over them.

Makes 4 to 6 servings

Herb Dumplings. In a large bowl, combine 2 cups (250 g) **all-purpose flour,** 4 teaspoons **baking powder,** ½ teaspoon **salt,** and ½ teaspoon **dried dill weed.** Using a pastry blender or 2 knives, cut in 5 tablespoons (70 g) firm **butter** or margarine until mixture resembles coarse meal. Lightly mix in 2 tablespoons chopped **parsley** and 2 tablespoons chopped **chives.** Make a well in center; pour in 1 cup (240 ml) **evaporated skim milk** all at once and stir with a fork until dough cleans sides of bowl.

Prep: *About 25 minutes*
Cook: *About 1 hour*

Per serving: 692 calories, 33 g total fat, 13 g saturated fat, 132 mg cholesterol, 1,233 mg sodium, 55 g carbohydrates, 4 g fiber, 43 g protein, 425 mg calcium, 5 mg iron

Baked sliced apples and plump golden raisins nestle under a crumbly topping flecked with sharp Cheddar cheese. Add scoops of vanilla frozen yogurt or ice cream to melt into the hot-from-the-oven dessert.

Apple-Cheese Crumble

4 large tart green-skinned apples such as Granny Smith (1¾ to 2 lbs./795 to 905 g total), peeled, cored, and sliced

¼ cup (35 g) golden raisins

½ cup (100 g) sugar

¾ teaspoon ground cinnamon

½ cup (60 g) all-purpose flour

2 tablespoons (30 g) cold butter or margarine

½ cup (55 g) shredded sharp Cheddar cheese

Vanilla frozen yogurt or ice cream (optional)

Spread apples in a 7- by 10-inch oval au gratin pan, 8-inch-square cake pan, or shallow 2-quart casserole. Stir in raisins, ¼ cup (50 g) of the sugar, and cinnamon; spread out evenly and set aside.

In a medium-size bowl, stir together flour and remaining ¼ cup (50 g) sugar. Using a pastry blender or 2 knives, cut in butter and cheese until mixture resembles coarse meal. Sprinkle mixture evenly over apples.

Bake in a 350°F (175°C) oven until topping is golden and apples are tender when pierced (about 1 hour). Serve warm or at room temperature; top with frozen yogurt, if desired.

Makes 4 to 6 servings

Prep: *About 25 minutes*
Cook: *About 1 hour*

Per serving: *315 calories, 9 g total fat, 5 g saturated fat, 24 mg cholesterol, 119 mg sodium, 57 g carbohydrates, 3 g fiber, 5 g protein, 99 mg calcium, 1 mg iron*

Cooking tips: *To make an easy **Mulled Cranberry Cider** for 4 to 6 servings, start by pouring 1 can (about 12 oz./355 ml) **frozen cranberry-apple juice concentrate** into a 2½- or 3½-quart sauce pan. Dilute concentrate with **water** according to the label directions, substituting up to 2 cups (470 ml) dry red wine or fruit juice (such as white grape juice or orange juice) for an equal amount of water, if desired. Heat the cider until steaming hot; then add **clove-studded orange slices**, a **cinnamon stick**, and a few **whole allspice** or cardamom to taste. Let the mixture simmer for about 15 minutes to blend the spicy flavors.*

Spring Planting

*Gardening reawakens
appetites for foods long
absent from the winter
table—such spring delicacies
as asparagus, strawberries,
young lamb, and fresh herbs.
Here's a dinner menu that
makes the most of them.*

Five-onion Soup

Crusty French Bread

Wine-roasted Lamb & New
Potatoes with Basil Gremolata

Roasted Asparagus

Double-dipped Strawberries
Orange Butter Cookies

Coffee

Leeks, one of the milder-mannered members of the onion family, are joined by shallots, garlic, and red and yellow onions in this creamy first-course soup.

Five-onion Soup

2 large leeks (about 1 lb./ 455 g total)

1½ tablespoons (23 ml) olive oil

2 cloves garlic, minced

3 shallots (85 g total), finely chopped

1 medium-size yellow onion (about 6 oz./170 g), finely chopped

½ cup (85 g) finely chopped red onion

2 cups (470 ml) fat-free reduced-sodium chicken broth

⅔ cup (160 ml) dry white wine

1 small dried bay leaf

¼ teaspoon dried thyme

½ teaspoon white pepper

1 can (about 12 oz./355 ml) evaporated skim milk

Salt

Chopped parsley

Trim ends and most of green tops from leeks; remove tough outer leaves. Split leeks lengthwise; rinse well, then thinly slice crosswise. Set leeks aside.

Preheat a 2½- or 3½-quart sauce pan over medium heat until rim of pan is hot-to-the-touch. Add oil and wait for about 1 more minute. Add leeks, garlic, shallots, yellow onion, and red onion; reduce heat to medium-low. Cook, stirring often, until onions are very soft (15 to 20 minutes).

Stir in broth, wine, bay leaf, thyme, and pepper. Bring to a boil; then boil gently, stirring occasionally, until mixture is reduced by about a third (about 10 minutes). Reduce heat to low; stir in milk. Heat just until soup is steaming hot (about 5 minutes). Remove and discard bay leaf. Season to taste with salt. Sprinkle with parsley before serving.

Makes 4 servings

Prep: *About 30 minutes*
Cook: *35 to 40 minutes*

Per serving: *192 calories, 5 g total fat, 1 g saturated fat, 4 mg cholesterol, 407 mg sodium, 26 g carbohydrates, 2 g fiber, 11 g protein, 334 mg calcium, 2 mg iron*

Cooking tips: *When you shop for leeks, choose those with clean white bottoms and crisp, fresh-looking green tops. Small to medium-size leeks (less than 1½ inches/3.5 cm in diameter) are the most tender, with a mild, delicate flavor. Before slicing them, be sure to rinse them thoroughly to wash away any grit concealed between the layers.*

Use a dry white wine such as sauvignon blanc to moisten and flavor lamb and new potatoes as they roast; then use a bit more to enliven the citrus-accented sauce.

Wine-roasted Lamb & New Potatoes with Basil Gremolata

1   half-leg of lamb (3½ to
    4 lbs./1.6 to 1.8 kg),
    bone in

8   to 12 very small red thin-
    skinned potatoes (about
    1 lb./455 g total), each 1½
    to 2 inches (3.5 to 5 cm) in
    diameter

1½ cups (360 ml) dry white
    wine, such as sauvignon
    blanc

    Freshly ground pepper

    Basil Gremolata (recipe
    follows)

½   cup (120 ml) fat-free
    reduced-sodium chicken broth

1½ teaspoons cornstarch blended
    with 2 tablespoons (30 ml)
    cold water

    Salt

Trim and discard surface fat from lamb. Place lamb, bony side down, in an 11- by 14-inch roasting pan; insert a meat thermometer in thickest part. Scrub potatoes and cut into halves crosswise; surround lamb with potatoes, cut sides down. Pour 1 cup (240 ml) of the wine over lamb; grind pepper over lamb to taste. Roast in a 350°F (175°C) oven until meat thermometer registers 135° to 140°F (57° to 60°C) for medium-rare (1½ to 2 hours). Shortly before lamb is done, prepare Basil Gremolata and set aside.

Transfer lamb and potatoes to a platter and cover lightly with foil; keep warm. Skim and discard any fat from roasting pan. Pour in broth and remaining ½ cup (120 ml) wine; stir to scrape browned pan juices free. Blend in cornstarch mixture; then place pan over medium-high heat and cook, stirring constantly, until sauce boils and thickens. Stir in 1 tablespoon of the gremolata and season to taste with salt.

To serve, slice lamb. Sprinkle remaining gremolata over lamb and potatoes; serve with sauce to add to taste.

Makes 4 to 6 servings

Basil Gremolata. In a small bowl, combine 2 cloves **garlic** (minced), 1 tablespoon grated **orange zest**, 1 teaspoon grated **lemon zest**, and 10 large **fresh basil leaves** (cut into fine ribbons). Mix lightly.

Prep: *About 20 minutes*
Cook: *1½ to 2 hours*

Per serving: *380 calories, 10 g total fat, 4 g saturated fat, 139 mg cholesterol, 204 mg sodium, 19 g carbohydrates, 2 g fiber, 47 g protein, 30 mg calcium, 5 mg iron*

Cooking tips: *When roasting a large cut of meat, the most accurate indicator of doneness is a meat thermometer inserted in the thickest part of the roast. Many cooks prefer their lamb cooked medium-rare to medium, but if you like it well done, roast it to an internal temperature of about 170°F (75°C).*

Balsamic vinegar adds a sweet-tart finishing touch to slender asparagus spears roasted in a very hot oven (cook them after the lamb is done, while you're making the sauce). To retain the spring-green color of the asparagus, add the vinegar at the very last minute—just before serving.

Roasted Asparagus

1½ pounds (680 g) very slender
   asparagus (about ¼ inch/
   6 mm in diameter)
1 tablespoon (15 ml) olive oil
   Salt and freshly ground
   pepper
2 tablespoons (30 ml)
   balsamic vinegar
¼ cup (15 g) Parmesan cheese
   curls

Place a 10-inch omelette pan in a 500°F (260°C) oven for 5 minutes. Meanwhile, snap off and discard tough ends of asparagus; then set asparagus aside.

Pour oil into pan and swirl to coat pan bottom evenly; then use tongs to roll asparagus in oil. Return pan to oven and bake until asparagus is tender-crisp to bite (5 to 7 minutes).

Season to taste with salt and pepper. Just before serving, drizzle with vinegar and sprinkle with cheese.

Makes 4 servings

Prep: *About 10 minutes*
Cook: *10 to 12 minutes*

Per serving: *75 calories, 5 g total fat, 1 g saturated fat, 2 mg cholesterol, 60 mg sodium, 5 g carbohydrates, 1 g fiber, 5 g protein, 72 mg calcium, 1 mg iron*

Cooking tips: *To make thin shavings of Parmesan cheese that curl slightly, bring a chunk of cheese to room temperature; then slowly pull a vegetable peeler across it.*

This simple, luscious dessert calls for the biggest, reddest berries you can find—preferably with the stems still attached. Plan to use the berries within a day or two of purchase, and wait to rinse them until shortly before serving.

Double-dipped Strawberries

16 to 20 large strawberries
with stems (about
1½ lbs./680 g total)

About ½ cup (120 ml) orange
muscat or black
muscat dessert wine

About ½ cup (100 g)
powdered sugar

Rinse strawberries, but do not remove hulls and stems. Let berries drain on paper towels, then place them in a bowl or basket. Pour wine into a small bowl; place powdered sugar in another small bowl (or divide it among 4 small individual dishes). Let each person dip berries, one at a time, first into wine, then into powdered sugar.

Makes 4 servings

Prep: *About 10 minutes*

Per serving: *152 calories, 1 g total fat, 0 g saturated fat, 0 mg cholesterol, 4 mg sodium, 30 g carbohydrates, 4 g fiber, 1 g protein, 25 mg calcium, 1 mg iron*

Cooking tips: *For flavor variety, you can also use orange-flavored liqueur or bourbon as a dip for the strawberries; or try an off-dry white wine such as a chenin blanc or California Riesling.*

The intense orange flavor of these traditional buttery cutouts is a pleasant complement to strawberries or any other favorite fresh berries, in spring and throughout the summer.

Orange Butter Cookies

½ cup (4 oz./115 g) butter or margarine, at room temperature

¼ cup (100 g) granulated sugar

1 teaspoon grated orange zest

1 large egg yolk

½ teaspoon vanilla

1½ cups (185 g) all-purpose flour

¾ cup (90 g) powdered sugar

1½ tablespoons (23 ml) orange juice

In a large bowl, combine butter and granulated sugar; beat with an electric mixer until creamy and well blended. Beat in ½ teaspoon of the orange zest, egg yolk, and vanilla. Gradually mix in flour, beating at low speed until dough is well combined.

On a lightly floured board, roll out dough about ⅛ inch (3 mm) thick. Cut out with floured decorative cutters about 2 inches (5 cm) wide. Place cookies slightly apart on a lightly greased medium-size cookie sheet. Gather scraps of dough into a ball; reroll and cut again.

Bake cookies in a 350°F (175°C) oven until pale gold all over and lightly browned at edges (about 15 minutes). Transfer to racks to cool.

In a small bowl, blend powdered sugar and orange juice until smooth. Stir in remaining ½ teaspoon orange zest. Spread or brush glaze over cookies; let stand until glaze is set (about 10 minutes).

Makes about 2½ dozen cookies

Prep: *About 20 minutes, plus about 30 minutes to cool*
Cook: *About 15 minutes*

Per cookie: *73 calories, 3 g total fat, 2 g saturated fat, 15 mg cholesterol, 32 mg sodium, 10 g carbohydrates, 0.2 g fiber, 1 g protein, 3 mg calcium, 0.3 mg iron*

Cooking tips: *Orange zest for use in cooking can be removed from the fruit with a citrus zester, a grater, a vegetable peeler, or a small, sharp paring knife. Always be sure to remove only the colored part of the peel, where the true citrus flavor is found; the white part beneath is likely to taste bitter.*

Weekend at the Cabin

.... 🌰 ....

*Even in the most rustic
setting, a touch of elegance
at the dinner table is
inviting. This menu is fairly
quick to put together with
groceries you bring
from home.*

**Quick Barley & White Bean Soup
with Prosciutto**

🌿

**Lemon Grilled Top Sirloin with
Portabellas & Cherry Tomatoes**

Potatoes Dijon

Garlic Sautéed Swiss Chard

🌿

**Pecan Bread Pudding with
Bourbon Sauce**

Red Wine   Coffee

This hearty soup is ready in a jiffy: barley cooks faster than you might think (in just half an hour), and the beans are canned. We suggest serving it as a first course, but when teamed with crusty bread and your choice of cheeses, it's also a good, warming main dish for lunch or supper.

Quick Barley & White Bean Soup with Prosciutto

2 tablespoons (30 g) butter or margarine

2 shallots (55 g total), finely chopped

1 medium-size carrot (about 2 oz./55 g), coarsely shredded

⅔ cup (115 g) pearl barley

5 cups (1.2 liters) fat-free reduced-sodium chicken broth

2 ounces (55 g) thinly sliced prosciutto, cut into thin strips

½ teaspoon dried thyme

¼ teaspoon pepper

1 can (about 15 oz./430 g) small white beans, rinsed and drained

Chopped parsley

Preheat a 2½- or 3½-quart sauce pan over medium-high heat until rim of pan is hot-to-the-touch. Add butter and wait for about 1 more minute. Add shallots and carrot; cook, stirring often, just until shallots are soft (about 3 minutes). Add barley; cook, stirring, until light golden. Stir in broth, prosciutto, thyme, and pepper. Bring to a boil; then reduce heat, cover, and simmer until barley is tender to bite (about 30 minutes).

Add beans; cook, stirring occasionally, until heated through (about 3 minutes). Sprinkle with parsley before serving.

Makes 4 to 6 servings

Prep: *About 15 minutes*
Cook: *About 45 minutes*

Per serving: *222 calories, 7 g total fat, 3 g saturated fat, 22 mg cholesterol, 962 mg sodium, 29 g carbohydrates, 6 g fiber, 12 g protein, 35 mg calcium, 2 mg iron*

Cooking tips: *Barley is a versatile grain to keep on hand in the pantry of your weekend or vacation home. Delicious in substantial soups like this one, it can also be used in place of rice in a cold salad or a hot, onion-accented pilaf. You can even cook it to serve as a hot breakfast cereal sweetened with brown sugar or maple syrup.*

If you like, start this savory side dish at home: cook the diced potatoes and mix them with the sour cream and mustard. At your destination, you need only spread the mixture in an au gratin pan and bake until hot and bubbling.

Potatoes Dijon

4   medium-size russet potatoes (1¾ to 2 lbs./795 to 905 g total)

1½ tablespoons (23 ml) olive oil

1   tablespoon butter or margarine

¼   cup (60 ml) reduced-fat sour cream

2   teaspoons Dijon mustard

1   tablespoon chopped chives
    Salt and freshly ground pepper

2   tablespoons chopped parsley

Peel and dice potatoes. Preheat a 12-inch omelette pan or 3-quart sauté pan over medium heat until rim of pan is hot-to-the-touch. Add oil and butter and wait for about 1 more minute. Add potatoes and cook, lightly stirring often, until golden brown and almost tender when pierced (15 to 20 minutes). Meanwhile, in a large bowl, combine sour cream, mustard, and chives; stir until blended.

Remove potatoes from heat and let cool for about 5 minutes. Then add to sour cream mixture and mix lightly to coat well. Season to taste with salt and pepper. (At this point, you may cover and refrigerate for up to 24 hours.)

Spread potato mixture evenly in a lightly greased 7- by 10-inch oval au gratin pan or 8-inch-square cake pan. Bake in a 350°F (175°C) oven until mixture is bubbling and golden brown on top (about 20 minutes; 25 to 35 minutes if refrigerated). Sprinkle with parsley before serving.

Makes 4 servings

Prep: *About 20 minutes*
Cook: *40 to 50 minutes*

Per serving: *253 calories, 10 g total fat, 3 g saturated fat, 13 mg cholesterol, 113 mg sodium, 36 g carbohydrates, 3 g fiber, 5 g protein, 4 mg calcium, 1 mg iron*

Cooking tips: *To make* **Garlic Sautéed Swiss Chard** *for 4 servings, start with 1 large bunch (about 1 lb./455 g)* **red Swiss chard.** *Rinse it well; cut out the stems and thick center ribs. Slice the stems and coarsely chop the leaves, keeping stems and leaves separate. Preheat a 3-quart sauté pan over medium-high heat until rim of pan is hot-to-the-touch. Add 2 tablespoons (30 ml)* **olive oil** *and wait for about 1 more minute. Add chard stems, 2 cloves* **garlic** *(minced), ⅛ teaspoon* **crushed red pepper flakes,** *and ¼ cup (60 ml)* **water;** *cover and cook over medium heat until stems are soft (5 to 8 minutes). Then stir in chard leaves; cook, stirring occasionally, until leaves are tender to bite (5 to 8 more minutes) and liquid has evaporated. Season to taste with* **salt** *and freshly ground* **pepper.**

To save precious weekend time, start the steak marinating (sealed in a plastic bag in the refrigerator) the night before you leave for your cabin. For best browning, remove the meat from the refrigerator (and set the marinade aside) 15 to 20 minutes before you're ready to cook.

Lemon Grilled Top Sirloin with Portabellas & Cherry Tomatoes

3 tablespoons (45 ml) lemon juice

2 tablespoons (30 ml) olive oil

½ teaspoon dried oregano

¼ teaspoon pepper

1 clove garlic, minced or pressed

1½ pounds (680 g) boneless top sirloin steak (about 1 inch/ 2.5 cm thick), trimmed of fat

1 cup (170 g) halved red and yellow cherry tomatoes

2 green onions, thinly sliced

2 tablespoons (30 g) butter or margarine

6 ounces (170 g) portabella or crimini mushrooms, sliced

Salt

In a large, heavy self-sealing plastic bag, combine lemon juice, oil, oregano, pepper, and garlic; shake to blend well. Place steak in bag; seal bag, then turn to coat steak on all sides. Refrigerate for at least 3 hours or up to 24 hours.

About 15 to 20 minutes before cooking steak, remove it from bag and set aside; reserve marinade. Just before cooking steak, combine tomatoes and onions in a small bowl; set aside.

Preheat an 11-inch-square or 12-inch-round grill pan over medium-high heat until rim of pan is hot-to-the-touch. Rub pan with about 1 teaspoon of the butter and wait for about 1 more minute. Place steak in pan and cook until well browned on bottom (about 6 minutes); turn steak over, then reduce heat to medium. Continue to cook until steak is well browned on second side and done to your liking; cut in thickest part to test (about 6 more minutes for medium-rare).

Meanwhile, heat a 10-inch omelette pan or 3-quart sauté pan over medium-high heat until rim of pan is hot-to-the-touch. Add remaining 5 teaspoons butter and wait for about 1 more minute. Add mushrooms and cook, stirring often, until tender and lightly browned (about 5 minutes). Add reserved marinade; cook until almost all liquid has evaporated.

Place steak on a serving board or platter; cut across the grain into thin slanting slices. Spoon mushrooms over servings of steak; season to taste with salt. Garnish with tomato mixture.

Makes 4 to 6 servings

Prep: *About 20 minutes, plus at least 3 hours to marinate*
Cook: *15 to 20 minutes*

Per serving: *286 calories, 16 g total fat, 6 g saturated fat, 95 mg cholesterol, 132 mg sodium, 5 g carbohydrates, 1 g fiber, 30 g protein, 22 mg calcium, 4 mg iron*

Luscious and custardy, this rich dessert is a dreamy conclusion to a long day in the frosty outdoors.

Pecan Bread Pudding with Bourbon Sauce

5   *large eggs*

1   *cup (200 g) sugar*

1   *teaspoon vanilla*

$^1/_8$ *teaspoon ground nutmeg*

$2^3/_4$ *cups (650 ml) low-fat (1%) milk*

4   *cups (about 4 oz./115 g) cubed day-old French bread*

$^1/_3$ *cup (40 g) coarsely chopped pecans*

$^1/_4$ *cup (30 g) dried currants*

$^1/_4$ *cup (55 g) butter or margarine, melted*

   Bourbon Sauce (recipe follows)

In a large bowl, beat eggs and sugar until well blended. Blend in vanilla and nutmeg, then stir in milk. Add bread, pecans, and currants; let stand for about 10 minutes, stirring often to saturate bread with egg mixture. Spoon bread mixture into a lightly greased 10-inch paella pan, 8-inch-square cake pan, or shallow 2-quart casserole. Drizzle with butter.

Set pan of pudding in a larger baking pan that is at least 2 inches (5 cm) deep; then set pans on middle rack of a 350°F (175°C) oven. Pour boiling water into larger pan to a depth of about 1 inch (2.5 cm). Bake until a knife inserted in center of pudding comes out clean (about 1 hour).

Serve pudding warm. Shortly before serving, prepare Bourbon Sauce. Serve warm sauce in a small pitcher or bowl to pour over pudding to taste.

Makes 4 to 6 servings

Bourbon Sauce. Melt $^1/_4$ cup (55 g) **butter** or margarine in a 1- or 1$^1/_2$-quart sauce pan over medium heat. Stir in $^1/_2$ cup (60 g) **powdered sugar** and $^1/_4$ cup (60 ml) **bourbon.** Cook, stirring, until sugar is dissolved. Reduce heat to low. In a small bowl, beat 1 large **egg yolk.** Stir in a little of the hot butter mixture; then return egg mixture to pan and cook, stirring constantly, until sauce is thickened (1 to 2 minutes). Remove from heat.

Prep: *About 20 minutes*
Cook: *About 1 hour and 5 minutes*

Per serving: 663 calories, 31 g total fat, 15 g saturated fat, 310 mg cholesterol, 458 mg sodium, 76 g carbohydrates, 1 g fiber, 14 g protein, 225 mg calcium, 2 mg iron

Cooking tips: *The custardy mixture that holds this pudding together will have the best texture if the pudding is baked slowly. Placing the pudding pan in a water bath moderates the heat reaching the custard, letting it set evenly without curdling.*

To the Beach!

Along the coast or at the shore, picnicking on the beach is a cherished tradition. This portable feast is sure to please, whether you gather the clams and crabs from a seaside seafood shack or purchase them from a reliable provider nearer home.

Curried Clam Chowder

Crusty French Bread or Focaccia

Crab Boil with
Ginger Dip & Cayenne Rémoulade
Sauce

Sweet Corn Coblets

Lemon Cheesecake Wedges
Muscat or Seedless Grapes

Dry White Wine   Lemonade
Coffee

You can prepare this spicy soup almost entirely at home. Simmer it until all the vegetables are tender, then chill it. At the beach, mix in the clams, tomatoes, and chile when you reheat the chowder on a portable stove or over a campfire.

Curried Clam Chowder

1 tablespoon (15 ml) salad oil

¼ cup (40 g) minced shallots

1 tablespoon minced fresh ginger

2 teaspoons curry powder

4 cups (950 ml) fish stock or bottled clam juice

3 cups (710 ml) dry white wine

1 large red thin-skinned potato (about 10 oz./285 g), scrubbed and cut into ¼-inch (6-mm) cubes

4 medium-size carrots (about 8 oz./230 g total), cut lengthwise into quarters, then sliced ¼ inch (6 mm) thick

2 to 3 cups (1 to 1½ lbs./455 to 680 g) cooked clams with broth

3 medium-size pear-shaped (Roma-type) tomatoes (about 10 oz./285 g total), diced

1 small Anaheim or other fresh mild green chile (about 3 oz./85 g), seeded and minced; or ½ cup (75 g) finely chopped green bell pepper

Lemon wedges (optional)

Preheat a 4½-quart sauce pan over medium-high heat until rim of pan is hot-to-the-touch. Add oil and wait for about 1 more minute. Add shallots and ginger. Cook, stirring often, until shallots begin to soften (about 2 minutes). Then add curry powder and stir for 1 more minute. Pour in fish stock and wine; bring to a gentle boil over medium-high heat. Add potato and carrots; adjust heat so mixture boils gently. Cover and cook until potato is very tender when pierced (about 20 minutes).

Mix in clams and their broth, tomatoes, and chile. Reduce heat to low and cook, uncovered, for 20 more minutes. Serve with lemon wedges to squeeze into soup to taste, if desired.

Makes 8 servings

Prep: *About 30 minutes*
Cook: *About 1 hour*

Per serving: *122 calories, 3 g total fat, 0.3 g saturated fat, 20 mg cholesterol, 313 mg sodium, 15 g carbohydrates, 2 g fiber, 10 g protein, 70 mg calcium, 9 mg iron*

Cooking tips: *To make* **Sweet Corn Coblets** *for 8 servings, cut 4 medium-size ears* **corn** *(each about 7 inches/18 cm long) into ¾-inch (2-cm) rounds. Cook corn in* **boiling water** *in a 6½-quart sauce pan or 8-quart sauce pot just until kernels are tender-crisp to bite (2 to 3 minutes). Drain corn and arrange in a large heatproof bowl. In same cooking pan, combine ½ cup (120 ml)* **distilled white vinegar;** *1 small* **onion** *(about 3 oz./85 g), minced; 2 tablespoons* **sugar;** *¼ cup (55 g) chopped* **bottled roasted red peppers;** *1 teaspoon* **mustard seeds;** *1 teaspoon* **crushed red pepper flakes;** *and ¼ teaspoon* **salt.** *Bring vinegar mixture to a boil and cook, stirring, until sugar is dissolved; then pour over corn. Let stand until cool, spooning dressing over corn frequently. If made ahead, cover and refrigerate for up to 6 hours.*

Make this well-seasoned shellfish feast with the kind of crab most available where you live—substantial Dungeness from the West Coast or smaller blue crabs from the Atlantic or Gulf Coasts. Dip the cooked crab in a piquant sauce (we offer two choices).

Crab Boil with Ginger Dip & Cayenne Rémoulade Sauce

Ginger Dip (page 39)

Cayenne Rémoulade Sauce (recipe follows)

3   *pouches (about 1½ oz./ 45 g each) packaged crab or shrimp boil (or use ⅓ cup/ 50 g mustard seeds, ⅓ cup/ 35 g dill seeds, 1 tablespoon whole black peppercorns, 1 tablespoon crushed red pepper flakes, 1 tablespoon coriander seeds, and 6 dried bay leaves)*

3   *lemons, thinly sliced*

10 *thin slices peeled fresh ginger (each about ¾ inch/2 cm in diameter)*

2   *tablespoons salt*

6   *live Dungeness crabs (9 to 12 lbs./4 to 5.5 kg total) or 24 live blue crabs (about 8 lbs./3.6 kg total)*

Prepare Ginger Dip and Cayenne Rémoulade Sauce; set aside in covered containers.

Pour 8 to 10 quarts (8 to 10 liters) water into a 16-quart stock pot. Add crab boil, lemons, ginger, and salt. Bring to a rapid boil. Pick up each crab, holding at rear, and plunge it headfirst into water, filling pot with half the crabs. Adjust heat so water boils gently. Allow 15 to 20 minutes to cook Dungeness crabs, 5 to 10 minutes to cook smaller crabs (start timing when the last crab has been added and water has returned to a gentle boil). Using tongs, remove cooked crabs; let drain on a tray. Return water to a rapid boil; then cook remaining crabs as directed above.

To clean each crab, break off and discard triangular belly flap; then turn crab over and, starting from rear, pull firmly to lift off back of shell. Pull spongy gills from body and tiny paddles from front. Scoop out golden crab butter. Rinse body well.

To crack crab, twist off claws and legs; set aside. Using a heavy cracker, crack claws and legs along edges of shells. Cut body into halves or quarters, then extract meat from body, claws, and legs using a metal pick, small fork, or tip of a crab leg.

Makes 8 servings

Cayenne Rémoulade Sauce. In a food processor, combine ½ cup (110g) coarsely chopped **bottled roasted red peppers,** 1½ cups (360 ml) **mayonnaise,** 2 tablespoons sliced **green onion,** ¼ cup (40 g) chopped **dill pickles,** ½ teaspoon **ground red pepper** (cayenne), 1½ tablespoons (23 ml) **prepared horseradish,** 1½ tablespoons drained **capers,** and ⅓ cup (20 g) chopped **parsley.** Process until puréed. Cover and refrigerate for at least 1 hour. Makes about 2⅔ cups (630 ml).

Prep: About 45 minutes, plus at least 1 hour to chill Cayenne Rémoulade Sauce
Cook: 30 to 45 minutes

Per serving of crab: 106 calories, 1 g total fat, 0.2 g saturated fat, 72 mg cholesterol, 497 mg sodium, 1 g carbohydrates, 0 g fiber, 21 g protein, 57 mg calcium, 0.5 mg iron
Per tablespoon of Cayenne Rémoulade Sauce: 58 calories, 6 g total fat, 1 g saturated fat, 5 mg cholesterol, 78 mg sodium, 1 g carbohydrates, 0.1 g fiber, 0.1 g protein, 3 mg calcium, 0.1 mg iron

A tangy lemon-flavored dessert is always a popular conclusion to a seafood meal. These lemon cookies combine a cool-tasting cheesecake topping with a buttery nut crust.

Lemon Cheesecake Wedges

3 tablespoons (45 g) butter or margarine, at room temperature

¼ cup (55 g) firmly packed brown sugar

½ cup (60 g) all-purpose flour

½ cup (60 g) chopped pecans or walnuts

Cheesecake Topping (recipe follows)

In a food processor, combine butter, sugar, flour, and pecans; process until mixture clings together to form a dough (or combine ingredients in a bowl, then rub with your fingers until fine crumbs form; press firmly together). Press dough evenly into a 9-inch-round cake pan. Bake in a 350°F (175°C) oven until lightly browned (about 15 minutes).

Meanwhile, prepare Cheesecake Topping. Spread topping evenly over partially baked crust. Return to oven and continue to bake until topping looks set in center when pan is gently shaken (about 15 more minutes). Let cool in pan on a rack; then cover and refrigerate until firm (at least 1 hour) or for up to 2 days. Use a thin spatula to loosen edge of crust, then carefully lift uncut round of cheesecake from pan. To serve, cut into 12 wedges.

Cheesecake Topping. In a food processor, combine 1 large package (about 8 oz./ 230 g) **Neufchâtel cheese** (at room temperature), ⅔ cup (135 g) **sugar**, 1 large **egg**, 1 tablespoon (15 ml) **lemon juice**, 2 teaspoons grated **lemon zest**, and ½ teaspoon **vanilla**; process until mixture is smooth. (Or combine ingredients in a large bowl and beat with an electric mixer until smooth.)

Makes 1 dozen cookies

Prep: *About 15 minutes, plus at least 1¼ hours to cool and chill*
Cook: *About 30 minutes*

Per cookie: *191 calories, 11 g total fat, 5 g saturated fat, 40 mg cholesterol, 112 mg sodium, 21 g carbohydrates, 0.4 g fiber, 3 g protein, 24 mg calcium, 1 mg iron*

Cooking tips: *To make **Ginger Dip** for Crab Boil, in a small bowl, mix ½ cup (120 ml) **rice wine vinegar**, 3 tablespoons sliced **green onions**, 2 tablespoons minced **fresh ginger**, and 1½ teaspoons **sugar**; stir until sugar is dissolved.*

Tailgating

Satisfy a hungry crowd with robust fare like this tailgate banquet of plump grilled sausages, warm potato salad, and spicy simmered cabbage and apples. To keep foods hot en route, use an insulated casserole; or insulate your Calphalon pan filled with hot food by wrapping it in heavy foil, then in several layers of newspaper, and placing it in a thermal bag.

Mustardy Sausage Sandwiches on
French Rolls

Spiced Red Cabbage

German Potato Salad

Chocolate Chip Cake

Beer   Soft Drinks   Coffee

Warm potato salad, smoky with bacon and mildly tangy with vinegar, is always a popular companion to plump, juicy sausages.

German Potato Salad

3 pounds (1.35 kg) medium-size red thin-skinned potatoes, scrubbed

6 ounces (170 g) sliced bacon

1 medium-size yellow onion (about 6 oz./170 g), finely chopped

1 cup (115 g) sliced celery

⅔ cup (160 ml) distilled white vinegar

⅓ cup (80 ml) water

1 tablespoon sugar

1 teaspoon salt

4 hard-cooked large eggs, sliced
    Salt and freshly ground pepper

In an 8-quart stock pot or sauce pot, bring about 4 quarts (3.8 liters) water to a boil over high heat. Add unpeeled potatoes; reduce heat, cover, and boil gently until potatoes are tender throughout when pierced (25 to 30 minutes). Drain and let stand until cool enough to touch. Peel potatoes, if desired; then cut into about ¾-inch (2-cm) chunks.

Meanwhile, preheat a 5-quart sauté pan over medium-high heat until rim of pan is hot-to-the-touch. Add bacon and cook, turning occasionally, until crisp and browned (6 to 8 minutes). Remove from pan; drain, crumble, and set aside. Discard all but 3 tablespoons (45 ml) of the drippings.

Return reserved drippings to pan and wait for about 1 more minute. Add onion and celery; reduce heat to medium and cook, stirring often, until vegetables are soft (8 to 10 minutes). Lightly mix in potatoes, then remove pan from heat and set aside.

In a 1½- or 2½-quart sauce pan, combine vinegar, the ⅓ cup (80 ml) water, sugar, and salt; bring to a boil over high heat. Pour vinegar mixture over potato mixture. Lightly mix in eggs and bacon. Season to taste with salt and pepper. Serve warm.

Makes 8 to 12 servings

Prep: *About 25 minutes*
Cook: *About 45 minutes*

Per serving: *211 calories, 8 g total fat, 2 g saturated fat, 92 mg cholesterol, 361 mg sodium, 29 g carbohydrates, 3 g fiber, 7 g protein, 20 mg calcium, 1 mg iron*

Cooking tips: *To take this warm potato salad to a tailgate picnic, prepare it up to the point of mixing the potatoes with the vinegar dressing, then wrap it to keep it warm as directed on page 41. Carry the cooked eggs and bacon in your cooler, then mix them into the salad just before serving.*

Perfect fare for a chilly-day repast (whether outdoors or in), this tempting sweet-tart vegetable dish is as good with grilled pork chops or pork roast as it is with sausages.

Spiced Red Cabbage

2 tablespoons (30 ml) vegetable oil

1 large head (about 2¼ lbs./ 1 kg) red cabbage, shredded

3 medium-size tart green-skinned apples such as Granny Smith (about 1 lb./455 g total), peeled, cored, and sliced

¼ cup (60 ml) red wine vinegar

½ cup (110 g) firmly packed brown sugar

1 teaspoon salt

¼ teaspoon ground cloves

¼ teaspoon pepper

½ teaspoon ground allspice

Preheat an 8-quart stock pot or sauce pot over medium-high heat until rim of pan is hot-to-the-touch. Add oil and wait for about 1 more minute. Reduce heat to medium and add cabbage. Cook, stirring often, until cabbage is soft (about 15 minutes).

Mix in apples, vinegar, sugar, salt, cloves, pepper, and allspice. Cover, reduce heat to low, and cook for 10 minutes. Then uncover and cook, stirring occasionally, until cabbage and apples are tender to bite (5 to 10 more minutes).

Makes 8 to 12 servings

Prep: About 20 minutes
Cook: About 35 minutes

Per serving: *116 calories, 3 g total fat, 0.4 g saturated fat, 0 mg cholesterol, 236 mg sodium, 23 g carbohydrates, 3 g fiber, 66 mg calcium, 1 mg iron*

Cooking tips: *Though it does contribute to the sweet-sour taste, the vinegar in this dish isn't only for flavor. It also helps to keep the red cabbage from taking on an unappetizing blue-purple color as it cooks.*

If you enjoy the smoky flavor of freshly grilled sausages when you tailgate, make the onion-mustard sauce at home and insulate it in the cooking pan. Then grill the sausages at your destination and add them to the sauce before serving.

Mustardy Sausage Sandwiches

3 tablespoons (45 ml)
   vegetable oil

5 large onions (about 2½ lbs./
   1.15 kg total), thinly sliced

2 cloves garlic, minced

4 to 6 bratwurst (about
   1½ lbs./680 g total); see
   Cooking tips

4 to 6 kielbasa (Polish
   sausages), about 1½ lbs./
   680 g total; see Cooking tips

3 tablespoons all-purpose flour

1½ cups (360 ml) fat-free
   reduced-sodium chicken broth

¼ cup (60 ml) catsup

¼ cup (60 ml) Dijon mustard

2 tablespoons (30 ml) prepared
   horseradish

8 to 12 French rolls (about
   2½ oz./70 g each), split and
   warmed

Preheat a 5-quart saucier pan or 4½- or 6½-quart sauce pan over medium-high heat until rim of pan is hot-to-the-touch. Add 2 tablespoons (30 ml) of the oil and wait for about 1 more minute. Mix in onions and garlic; reduce heat to medium, cover, and cook, stirring occasionally, until onions are very soft (about 10 minutes). Reduce heat to medium-low; uncover and cook, stirring often, until onions are golden (15 to 20 more minutes).

Meanwhile, heat an 11-inch-square or 12-inch-round grill pan over medium heat until rim of pan is hot-to-the-touch. Brush pan with remaining 1 tablespoon (15 ml) oil and wait for about 1 more minute. Add as many bratwurst and kielbasa as will fit in pan without crowding. Cook, turning as needed, until sausages are browned on all sides. As sausages are browned, remove from pan and keep warm.

When all sausages have been browned, stir flour into onion mixture. Gradually add broth; increase heat to medium and cook, stirring, until sauce boils and thickens. Blend in catsup, mustard, and horseradish. Cook, stirring often, until sauce is hot. Lightly mix sausages into sauce; spoon sausages and sauce into rolls. (Or place browned sausages in rolls direct from grill; spoon sauce over them.)

Makes 8 to 12 servings

Prep: *About 20 minutes*
Cook: *30 to 35 minutes*

Per serving: 715 calories, 43 g total fat, 14 g saturated fat, 86 mg cholesterol, 1,849 mg sodium, 53 g carbohydrates, 4 g fiber, 27 g protein, 140 mg calcium, 4 mg iron

Cooking tips: Much of the bratwurst and kielbasa on the market today is fully cooked —but if you choose uncooked sausages, here's how to precook them before grilling. Place the sausages in a pan large enough to hold them in a single layer; cover generously with water and bring to a boil over medium-high heat. Then remove from heat, cover, and let stand for 10 minutes. Drain well. (You can chill the precooked sausages for up to 8 hours before grilling.)

Chocolate, chocolate, and then a little more chocolate give this sweet, dark, moist cake a spectacularly rich flavor. It's perfect both at home and away.

Chocolate Chip Cake

¾ cup (6 oz./170 g) plus 1 tablespoon butter or margarine, at room temperature

¼ cup (30 g) sliced almonds

1 large package (about 12 oz./340 g) semisweet chocolate chips

1¾ cups (385 g) firmly packed brown sugar

3 large eggs

¾ cup (180 ml) reduced-fat sour cream

1 teaspoon vanilla

1½ cups (about 145 g) sifted cake flour

½ cup (43 g) unsweetened cocoa

1 teaspoon baking powder

½ teaspoon baking soda

¾ cup (180 ml) milk

1 teaspoon unsweetened cocoa (optional)

1 tablespoon powdered sugar (optional)

Use 1 tablespoon of the butter to grease a 10-inch crown BUNDT® pan; coat interior of pan evenly with almonds. Set pan aside. In a blender or food processor, process 1 cup (170 g) of the chocolate chips until finely ground; set ground chocolate aside.

In large bowl, beat remaining ¾ cup (170 g) butter and brown sugar with an electric mixer until creamy and blended. Add eggs, one at a time, beating until smooth and fluffy after each addition. Gradually blend in sour cream; then blend in vanilla and ground chocolate.

In a medium-size bowl, combine flour, the ½ cup (43 g) cocoa, baking powder, and baking soda; stir until well blended. Add flour mixture to butter mixture alternately with milk, beating until smooth after each addition. Stir in remaining 1 cup (170 g) chocolate chips.

Spread batter in prepared pan. Bake in a 350°F (175°C) oven until top of cake springs back when lightly touched and a wooden pick inserted in center of cake comes out clean (40 to 45 minutes). Let cool in pan on a rack for 30 minutes. Invert cake onto rack to cool completely. If desired, mix the 1 teaspoon cocoa and powdered sugar; sift over cake before cutting.

Makes 12 to 16 servings

Prep: *About 20 minutes, plus 30 minutes to cool*
Cook: *40 to 45 minutes*

Per serving: *415 calories, 22 g total fat, 12 g saturated fat, 81 mg cholesterol, 227 mg sodium, 55 g carbohydrates, 1 g fiber, 5 g protein, 84 mg calcium, 3 mg iron*

Cooking tips: *If you like, you can use your Calphalon Crown BUNDT® pan as a cake carrier as well as a baking pan. Turn the cake out onto a rack to cool as directed; then, once it's cool, carefully invert it back into the pan to protect it en route. Be sure to remove it from the pan again before cutting.*

Midsummer Barbecue

Smoky barbecued spareribs, well seasoned with a spicy sauce, rank high among favorite summer meals to share with family and friends. This menu works well as a potluck, with the host family providing the ribs and dessert.

Sticky Spicy Barbecued
Baby Back Ribs

Sweet & Sour Baked Beans

Green Apple & Cabbage Slaw

Carrot Corn Muffins   Honey

Strawberry Fool with Mixed
Berries & Shortbread Squares

Beer or Light Red Wine, such as
Beaujolais   Soft Drinks
Coffee

Pork loin back ribs, popularly known as baby back ribs, have less fat and are smaller than traditional pork spareribs. Lean and tender, they cook quickly on the barbecue.

Sticky Spicy Barbecued Baby Back Ribs

½ cup (120 ml) catsup

½ cup (120 ml) hoisin sauce

¼ cup (60 ml) lemon juice

¼ cup (50 g) sugar

4 cloves garlic, minced or pressed

½ teaspoon ground cinnamon

½ teaspoon ground allspice

¼ teaspoon ground red pepper (cayenne)

⅛ teaspoon ground cloves

About 6 pounds (2.7 kg) pork loin back ribs, trimmed of excess fat

In a medium-size bowl, combine catsup, hoisin sauce, lemon juice, sugar, garlic, cinnamon, allspice, red pepper, and cloves; mix well. Set aside. (At this point, you may cover and refrigerate sauce for up to 4 days.)

Place ribs on a grill 4 to 6 inches above a solid bed of medium-low coals. Cook, turning once, until browned on both sides (about 8 minutes per side). Transfer sauce to 2-cup sauce pan or butterwarmer and place at edge of grill. Brush ribs generously with sauce; continue to cook, turning as needed and brushing with sauce, until meat between bones is no longer pink (cut to test) and sauce is browned (6 to 10 more minutes). Cut into serving-size pieces.

Makes 8 servings

Prep: *About 10 minutes*
Cook: *About 25 minutes*

Per serving: *696 calories, 49 g total fat, 18 g saturated fat, 194 mg cholesterol, 661 mg sodium, 21 g carbohydrates, 0.3 g fiber, 40 g protein, 83 mg calcium, 2 mg iron*

Cooking tips: *To make **Carrot Corn Muffins,** prepare your favorite corn muffin recipe for 12 muffins. Stir ½ cup (55 g) finely shredded **carrot** (about 1 medium-size carrot) into liquid ingredients (mixture of milk, egg, and shortening) before adding liquid ingredients to flour mixture. You can also divide the muffin batter between 2 lightly greased 3- by 6-inch mini loaf pans; bake the loaves 3 to 5 minutes longer than the time indicated for muffins, or until a wooden skewer inserted in center comes out clean.*

Three kinds of beans go into this tangy, quickly assembled casserole. It's also good with barbecued chicken.

Sweet & Sour Baked Beans

4   ounces (115 g) sliced bacon

3   large onions (about 1¼ lbs./565 g total), thinly sliced

¾   cup (165 g) firmly packed brown sugar

⅓   cup (80 ml) cider vinegar

⅓   cup (80 ml) catsup

⅓   cup (80 ml) mild-flavored molasses

1   teaspoon dry mustard

2   cans (about 15 oz./450 g each) small white beans, rinsed and drained

1   can (about 15 oz./450 g) pinto or pink beans, rinsed and drained

1   can (about 15 oz./450 g) kidney beans, rinsed and drained

Preheat a 5-quart sauté pan over medium-high heat until rim of pan is hot-to-the-touch. Add bacon and cook, turning occasionally, until crisp and browned (6 to 8 minutes). Remove from pan; drain, crumble, and set aside. Discard all but 1 tablespoon of the drippings. Add onions to drippings. Stir in sugar and vinegar; cook, stirring occasionally, until liquid is reduced by half (about 10 minutes). Mix in catsup, molasses, and mustard; bring mixture to a boil, then remove pan from heat.

Add beans and bacon; stir gently until blended. (At this point, you may transfer mixture to a bowl, cover, and refrigerate for up to 24 hours.) Transfer mixture to a 2½-quart sauce pan with loop handles or a 3-quart chef's casserole. Cover and bake in a 350°F (175°C) oven until bean mixture is thick and sauce is rich tasting (about 2 hours).

Makes 8 to 10 servings

Prep: *About 15 minutes*
Cook: *About 2¼ hours*

Per serving: *252 calories, 4 g total fat, 1 g saturated fat, 4 mg cholesterol, 393 mg sodium, 48 g carbohydrates, 6 g fiber, 8 g protein, 85 mg calcium, 3 mg iron*

Cooking tips: *To make **Green Apple & Cabbage Slaw** for 8 servings, use any favorite creamy coleslaw recipe calling for 8 cups (750 g) shredded **green or napa cabbage**. Before adding dressing, core and dice 1 medium-large **tart green-skinned apple** such as Granny Smith (about 6 oz./170 g); mix into cabbage. For additional flavor, mix in about 2 tablespoons drained **pickled slivered ginger**. Then mix in dressing.*

A fool is a traditional English dessert that's almost absurdly easy to prepare: you just fold sweetened, slightly crushed fresh fruit into a bowl of whipped cream. This version is embellished with an array of multihued berries and dolloped atop buttery shortbread squares.

Strawberry Fool with Mixed Berries & Shortbread Squares

1 cup (125 g) all-purpose flour

¼ cup (32 g) cornstarch

¾ cup (90 g) powdered sugar

½ cup (4 oz./115 g) cold butter, diced

2 to 3 cups (300 to 450 g) strawberries, rinsed and patted dry

½ cup (100 g) granulated sugar

2 to 3 cups (290 to 435 g) mixed blackberries, blueberries, and raspberries, rinsed and patted dry

1 cup (240 ml) whipping cream

Mint sprigs (optional)

Sift flour, cornstarch, and powdered sugar into a large bowl. Add butter and mix to coat with flour mixture. Then rub mixture with your fingers until butter particles are very fine. Wrap dough in plastic wrap, using your hands to press it into a flattened ball (the warmth of your hands will melt butter enough to bring dough together). Place dough on an ungreased medium-size cookie sheet and cover it with the plastic wrap; then roll dough to form an 11- to 12-inch (28- to 30-cm) square. As you roll dough, reshape edges as needed. Discard plastic wrap.

Bake in a 300°F (150°C) oven until shortbread is pale golden (20 to 25 minutes). While shortbread is still on cookie sheet, use a nylon spatula to cut it into 9 equal squares. Let squares cool for about 5 minutes, then transfer to a large rack to cool.

Meanwhile, hull and chop about 2 cups of the strawberries (reserve remaining strawberries for garnish). Place chopped berries in a medium-size bowl and add sugar; set aside for 30 minutes. Using a fork, crush berries finely, mixing in any undissolved sugar.

In a chilled bowl, beat cream until stiff. Add crushed strawberry mixture, then fold in lightly until most of the crushed berries are mixed in. Transfer to a serving bowl. Hull remaining strawberries (and cut in half, if desired); garnish bowl of strawberry fool with strawberries and some of the mixed berries, using some of each kind. (Or, if desired, fold some of the mixed berries into the strawberry fool.) For each serving, place a cookie on a serving plate, top with a large dollop of the strawberry fool, and spoon on some of the remaining mixed berries. Garnish with mint sprigs, if desired.

Makes 8 servings

Prep: *About 30 minutes, plus 30 minutes for sweetened berries to stand*
Cook: *20 to 25 minutes*

Per serving: *399 calories, 23 g total fat, 14 g saturated fat, 72 mg cholesterol, 130 mg sodium, 47 g carbohydrates, 3 g fiber, 3 g protein, 42 mg calcium, 1 mg iron*

Picnic with
the Family

*Everyone loves fried chicken,
and it's an all-time favorite
for a family outing. Serve it
hot or cold, along with
tangy deviled eggs and a
cool couscous salad dotted
with vegetables and
dried fruits.*

Buttermilk Fried Chicken

Colorful Couscous Salad

Deviled Eggs with Olives

Traditional Pecan Pie

Assorted Fresh Fruit

Iced Tea

Be sure to package fried chicken carefully to prevent spoilage. Chicken to be served hot should be wrapped in foil while hot, then wrapped in insulating material such as newspapers. To serve chicken cold, refrigerate it until well chilled, then carry it in an insulated cooler.

Buttermilk Fried Chicken

2 to 2½ pounds (905 g to 1.15 kg) chicken pieces, such as breast halves, thighs, and/or drumsticks, skinned if desired

About ⅓ cup (80 ml) buttermilk

¾ cup (95 g) all-purpose flour

½ teaspoon salt

½ teaspoon paprika

⅛ teaspoon white pepper

½ cup (100 g) solid vegetable shortening

Rinse chicken and pat dry; set aside. Pour buttermilk into a shallow bowl. In another shallow bowl, mix flour, salt, paprika, and pepper. Dip chicken pieces, one at a time, in buttermilk until evenly moistened; then roll in flour mixture and shake off excess (reserve remaining flour mixture). Place pieces slightly apart on a cookie sheet and refrigerate, uncovered, for 1 hour.

Melt shortening in a 5-quart sauté pan over medium heat. Meanwhile, recoat chicken with remaining flour mixture; shake off excess. To test temperature of shortening, drop a pinch of flour into pan; flour should float and sizzle on hot fat. If flour sinks to bottom of pan and disperses, fat is not hot enough.

Arrange chicken pieces, bony sides up, in a single layer in hot fat. Allow enough space between pieces for fat to bubble and sizzle. Cook chicken for 10 minutes. Turn pieces over with tongs, cover, and cook for 20 more minutes. Then uncover and continue to cook, turning as needed, until coating is crisp and golden brown and meat near thighbone or in thickest part is no longer pink; cut to test (15 to 20 more minutes). Remove chicken from pan and drain on paper towels. Serve hot. Or, to serve cold, let cool; then refrigerate, uncovered, until chilled.

Makes 4 servings

Prep: *About 10 minutes, plus 1 hour for chicken to chill before cooking*
Cook: *45 to 50 minutes*

Per serving: *540 calories, 36 g total fat, 10 g saturated fat, 117 mg cholesterol, 403 mg sodium, 19 g carbohydrates, 1 g fiber, 32 g protein, 46 mg calcium, 3 mg iron*

Cooking tips: *The high, straight sides of a Calphalon sauté pan make it a good choice for frying chicken; it contains the fat, preventing spattering.*

Bits of crunchy vegetables and tart dried cherries, raisins, and apricots mingle with fluffy couscous in this cool salad. Superb with fried chicken, it's also a fine accompaniment to grilled meats such as lamb chops or teriyaki-marinated pork tenderloin.

Colorful Couscous Salad

Orange Dressing (recipe follows)

1   *tablespoon (15 ml) olive oil*

½   *teaspoon curry powder*

⅛   *teaspoon ground red pepper (cayenne)*

1¼ *cups (300 ml) fat-free reduced-sodium chicken broth*

1   *cup (185 g) couscous*

½   *cup (65 g) matchstick pieces dried apricots*

¼   *cup (35 g) dried cherries*

½   *cup (75 g) golden raisins*

1   *cup (145 g) frozen tiny peas*

½   *cup (75 g) chopped red bell pepper*

¼   *cup (40 g) finely chopped red onion*

Prepare Orange Dressing; cover and refrigerate while preparing couscous.

Preheat a 2½- or 3½-quart sauce pan over medium heat until rim of pan is hot-to-the-touch. Add oil and wait for about 1 more minute. Add curry powder and ground red pepper and stir for about 30 seconds. Add broth, increase heat to high, and bring to a boil. Stir in couscous, apricots, cherries, raisins, and peas; cover pan and remove from heat. Let stand until all liquid has been absorbed (about 5 minutes). Fluff couscous lightly with a fork; then stir in Orange Dressing, bell pepper, and onion.

Transfer couscous mixture to a large bowl, cover, and refrigerate until cold (at least 2 hours) or for up to 8 hours.

Makes 4 to 6 servings

Orange Dressing. In a small bowl, mix 2 teaspoons **Dijon mustard**, ½ cup (120 ml) **orange juice**, and 1 tablespoon (15 ml) **olive oil** until well combined. Then stir in 2 teaspoons grated **orange zest**, 1 teaspoon minced **crystallized ginger**, and 2 tablespoons chopped **parsley.**

Prep: About 20 minutes, plus at least 2 hours to chill
Cook: About 10 minutes

Per serving: 332 calories, 6 g total fat, 1 g saturated fat, 0 mg cholesterol, 248 mg sodium, 63 g carbohydrates, 6 g fiber, 9 g protein, 42 mg calcium, 2 mg iron

Cooking tips: Bring out the full, rich flavor of curry powder by cooking it in a little heated oil or butter before you combine it with additional ingredients.

Inventive packaging transforms even such basic picnic fare as deviled eggs into a treat few can resist!

Deviled Eggs with Olives

4   large eggs

2   tablespoons (30 ml) mayonnaise

1   teaspoon Dijon mustard

1/8 teaspoon paprika

1/4 cup (35 g) chopped pimento-stuffed green olives

Salt and freshly ground pepper

1/4 cup (15 g) finely chopped parsley

Fill a 1½-quart sauce pan three-fourths full of water. Place over high heat. When water shows the first signs of a rolling boil, reduce heat so that only an occasional bubble glides upward from pan bottom. Add eggs; adjust heat to keep water barely bubbling. Cook for 12 minutes; then immediately plunge eggs into cold water to stop them cooking.

When eggs are cool, shell them and cut in half crosswise. Carefully remove egg yolks and place in a small bowl; set egg white halves aside in an empty egg carton. With a fork, mash yolks; stir in mayonnaise, mustard, and paprika. Then stir in olives. Season to taste with salt and pepper.

Generously fill egg white halves with yolk mixture. For each serving, sandwich 2 egg halves together so a little filling is squeezed out at cut edges; then roll in parsley to define edge. Wrap each serving in plastic wrap, twisting ends so wrapped egg resembles a bonbon. Refrigerate until eggs are cold (at least 1 hour) or for up to 6 hours.

Makes 4 servings

Prep: *About 20 minutes, plus at least 1 hour to chill*
Cook: *About 15 minutes*

Per serving: *139 calories, 12 g total fat, 3 g saturated fat, 217 mg cholesterol, 337 mg sodium, 1 g carbohydrates, 0.4 g fiber, 7 g protein, 36 mg calcium, 1 mg iron*

Cooking tips: *Though most of us think of them as hard "boiled," hard-cooked eggs will have a more tender texture, a better flavor, and a more attractive color if you don't actually cook them at a full, rolling boil. Instead, regulate the heat so the eggs cook in water that never exceeds 200°F (95°C)—a temperature at which only an occasional bubble glides upward from the pan bottom. To preserve the golden color of the yolks, immediately immerse the cooked eggs in cold water to stop cooking.*

Ask people to name their favorite pies, and pecan pie is likely to be high on the list. With or without whipped cream, this bourbon-accented version is irresistible.

Traditional Pecan Pie

Pastry for a single-crust 9-inch (23-cm) pie

3 *large eggs*

³⁄₄ *cup (165 g) firmly packed brown sugar*

1 *cup (240 ml) light corn syrup*

¹⁄₈ *teaspoon salt*

1 *tablespoon (15 ml) bourbon*

1 *tablespoon butter or margarine, melted*

1 *cup (115 g) pecan halves*

Unsweetened whipped cream (optional)

On a lightly floured board, roll pastry into an 11½-inch (29-cm) round; fit into cover of a 2½-quart Calphalon casserole with loop handles or into a 9-inch (23-cm) pie pan. Trim and flute edge.

In a large bowl, beat eggs, sugar, corn syrup, salt, bourbon, and butter until well blended. Stir in pecans. Pour filling into pastry shell.

Bake in a 375°F (190°C) oven until pastry is golden brown and filling looks set in center when pan is gently shaken (45 to 50 minutes). Let cool on a rack for at least 2 hours before serving. Top with whipped cream, if desired.

Makes 8 servings

Prep: *About 15 minutes, plus at least 2 hours to cool*
Cook: *45 to 50 minutes*

Per serving: *446 calories, 20 g total fat, 4 g saturated fat, 84 mg cholesterol, 248 mg sodium, 65 g carbohydrates, 1 g fiber, 5 g protein, 36 mg calcium, 2 mg iron*

Cooking tips: *The cover of a 2½-quart Calphalon Professional Hard-Anodized casserole measures 8 inches in diameter and can be used as a pie pan. The covers of the larger casseroles (5-, 8½-, and 15-quart sizes) can also be used to bake quiches and vegetable gratins.*

Super Bowl Sunday

Super Bowl Sunday has become a well-established occasion for a no-holds-barred party featuring finger foods galore, along with such hot and hearty dishes as the ample chili in this menu.

Hot Artichoke Dip

Toasted Baguette Slices
Crisp Raw Vegetables

Spicy Chicken Wings

Celery Sticks   Blue Cheese Dip

Jim's Super Hot Chili

Assorted Condiments

Truffle Brownies

Cold Beer   Coffee

Use toasted baguette slices to scoop up this warm, creamy dip. Or try pita crisps, made by brushing triangles of split pita bread with a little olive oil and baking them on a cookie sheet in a 350°F (175°C) oven until golden brown (10 to 12 minutes).

Hot Artichoke Dip

1 long, slender baguette (about 8 oz./230 g; about 25 inches/63 cm long), cut diagonally into 32 slices

1 cup (about 3 oz./85 g) grated Parmesan cheese

1 large package (about 8 oz./ 230 g) Neufchâtel cheese or regular cream cheese, at room temperature

1 cup (240 ml) reduced-fat sour cream or reduced-calorie mayonnaise

1/8 teaspoon dried dill weed

1 can (about 14 oz./400 g) artichoke hearts, drained and chopped

Crisp raw vegetables, such as broccoli flowerets, diagonally sliced carrots, diagonally sliced zucchini or crookneck squash, and bell pepper strips

Arrange baguette slices in a single layer on large cookie sheets. Bake in a 325°F (165°C) oven until crisp and tinged with brown (15 to 20 minutes). Transfer toast to a rack to cool.

Meanwhile, set aside 1 tablespoon of the Parmesan cheese. In a large bowl, combine remaining Parmesan cheese, Neufchâtel cheese, sour cream, and dill weed. Beat with an electric mixer until smooth. Stir in artichokes. (At this point, you may cover and refrigerate for up to 24 hours.) Divide mixture between two 2-cup soup/soufflé pans; or spoon it into a single 1-quart baking dish. Sprinkle with reserved 1 tablespoon Parmesan cheese.

Bake, uncovered, in a 325°F (165°C) oven until dip is bubbly and lightly browned (30 to 35 minutes; 40 to 45 minutes if refrigerated). Serve with toast and vegetables.

Makes 8 servings

Prep: *About 10 minutes*
Cook: *45 to 55 minutes*

Per serving: *261 calories, 15 g total fat, 8 g saturated fat, 40 mg cholesterol, 500 mg sodium, 20 g carbohydrates, 1 g fiber, 12 g protein, 197 mg calcium, 1 mg iron*

Cooking tips: *Neufchâtel is a lighter form of cream cheese that contains less butterfat than the regular product. You can substitute it for cream cheese in most recipes, for a substantial savings in calories from fat.*

Just one of these tangy chicken wings is never enough—but fortunately, the recipe is so generous that the crowd can keep coming back for more.

Spicy Chicken Wings with Blue Cheese Dip

4 pounds (1.8 kg) chicken wings, cut apart at joints

Red Hot Sauce (recipe follows)

Blue Cheese Dip (recipe follows)

1 large bunch celery (1½ to 2 lbs./680 to 905 g)

Discard chicken wingtips (or reserve to make stock). Rinse remaining wing pieces and pat dry, then arrange in a single layer in a lightly greased 13- by 18-inch jelly roll pan. Bake in a 400°F (205°C) oven until golden brown (about 30 minutes).

Meanwhile, prepare Red Hot Sauce. Remove pan from oven, drain off and discard fat, and pour sauce over chicken; turn chicken to coat well. Then continue to bake, uncovered, turning wings once or twice, until sauce is bubbly and edges of wings are crisp (about 15 more minutes).

Meanwhile, prepare Blue Cheese Dip. Then break celery stalks from bunch; remove and discard leaves. Rinse stalks and slice lengthwise; then cut crosswise into sticks of a good length for dipping. Place in a serving bowl. Arrange chicken on a platter. Offer with celery sticks and Blue Cheese Dip.

Red Hot Sauce. In a small bowl, stir together ½ cup (120 ml) **distilled white vinegar,** ½ cup (120 ml) **water,** ¼ cup (60 ml) **tomato paste,** 4 teaspoons **sugar,** 2 tablespoons (30 ml) **liquid hot pepper seasoning,** and 1 to 3 teaspoons **ground red pepper** (cayenne).

Blue Cheese Dip. In a bowl, coarsely mash 4 ounces (115 g) **blue-veined cheese.** Stir in 1 cup (240 ml) **sour cream,** 1 teaspoon minced **garlic,** ½ teaspoon **dry mustard,** and ⅛ teaspoon **pepper.** If made ahead, cover and refrigerate for up to 3 days. Makes about 1⅓ cups.

Makes 8 servings (about 4 dozen appetizers)

Prep: About 25 minutes
Cook: About 45 minutes

Per appetizer without dip: *47 calories, 3 g total fat, 1 g saturated fat, 12 mg cholesterol, 52 mg sodium, 1 g carbohydrates, 0.3 g fiber, 4 g protein, 9 mg calcium, 0.3 mg iron*

Per tablespoon of Blue Cheese Dip: *43 calories, 4 g total fat, 2 g saturated fat, 9 mg cholesterol, 81 mg sodium, 1 g carbohydrates, 0 g fiber, 2 g protein, 42 mg calcium, 0 mg iron*

To boost the heat level of this full-flavored chili, choose the spicy kind or an unseasoned variety of kidney beans. For those who prefer their chili still hotter, provide chopped fresh jalapeños in the assortment of condiments.

Jim's Super Hot Chili

2 tablespoons (30 ml) olive oil

1 clove garlic, minced

3 pounds (1.35 kg) lean ground beef

1 large onion (about 8 oz./ 230 g), diced

1 large green bell pepper (about 8 oz./230 g), seeded and chopped

1 tablespoon ground cumin

3 tablespoons chili powder

2 teaspoons ground red pepper (cayenne)

1 teaspoon dried oregano

3 dried bay leaves

1 large can (about 28 oz./ 794 g) diced tomatoes

3 cans (about 8 oz./230 g each) tomato sauce

1 large can (about 27 oz./ 765 g) spicy red kidney beans or unseasoned red kidney beans

Salt and freshly ground pepper

Condiments (see Cooking tips)

Preheat a 5-quart saucier pan over medium-high heat until rim of pan is hot-to-the-touch. Add oil and wait for about 1 more minute. Add garlic and stir until it begins to color (about 30 seconds). Crumble in beef; then add onion, bell pepper, cumin, chili powder, red pepper, and oregano. Cook, stirring occasionally, until meat is browned. Spoon off and discard excess fat.

Stir in bay leaves, tomatoes and their liquid, tomato sauce, and beans and their liquid. Bring mixture to a boil; then reduce heat and simmer, uncovered, stirring occasionally, until chili is slightly thickened (30 to 45 minutes). Remove and discard bay leaves. Season to taste with salt and pepper.

Ladle chili into bowls. Offer condiments to add to taste.

Makes 8 servings

Prep: *About 20 minutes*
Cook: *45 to 50 minutes*

Per serving: *522 calories, 28 g total fat, 10 g saturated fat, 103 mg cholesterol, 1,134 mg sodium, 31 g carbohydrates, 10 g fiber, 38 g protein, 106 mg calcium, 6 mg iron*

Cooking tips: *Offer small bowls of condiments to add individuality to each fan's serving of chili. Suggestions include coarsely crushed **corn chips,** diced **cucumber,** shredded **Cheddar cheese, sour cream,** and seeded, chopped **fresh green or red jalapeño chiles.** For another distinctive topping, mix matchstick pieces of **radish** with strands of **orange zest** and moisten with **seasoned rice vinegar.***

*Create **Truffle Brownies** by adding 8 ounces (230 g) **chocolate truffles** to your favorite basic brownie recipe that bakes in an 8- or 9-inch-square cake pan. Use any flavor of truffles with solid centers; if truffles are very large, cut them into 1-inch (2.5-cm) chunks. Stir in the truffle pieces when you add the flour to the brownie batter.*

Casual Dinner Party

Mussels in a sauce you can't resist mopping up with crusty bread, orange-accented chicken paired with pasta, a salad of baby spinach in a fresh pineapple dressing— casual dishes like these add up to a dinner party menu sure to please your friends.

Steamed Mussels with
Tomatoes & Garlic

Crusty French or Italian Bread

Fresh Spinach Salad with
Pineapple & Honey Dressing

Chicken Valencia

Fettuccine Lucchese

Peaches with Caramel &
Black Pepper Sauce

Dry White Wine, such as
Pinot Grigio   Espresso Coffee

Look for small cultivated blue mussels to use in this delectable first course. If you have any leftover cooked mussels, remove them from the shells and refrigerate them in the sauce—you'll have a splendid pasta sauce for tomorrow's supper.

Steamed Mussels with Tomatoes & Garlic

¼ cup (60 ml) olive oil

1 large onion (about 8 oz./ 230 g), finely chopped

3 large tomatoes (about 1½ lbs./680 g total), seeded and chopped

1½ tablespoons (23 ml) tomato paste

¾ cup (180 ml) dry white wine

1 cup (240 ml) fish stock or bottled clam juice

Salt and freshly ground pepper

3 pounds (1.35 kg) mussels in shell, scrubbed

2 cloves garlic, minced

3 tablespoons chopped parsley

Preheat a 2- or 3-quart sauté pan over medium-high heat until rim of pan is hot-to-the-touch. Add 2 tablespoons (30 ml) of the oil and wait for about 1 more minute. Add onion and cook, stirring occasionally, until soft and beginning to brown (3 to 5 minutes). Add tomatoes and tomato paste; continue to cook, stirring often, for 5 minutes. Pour in wine and cook, stirring occasionally, until mixture is reduced by half (about 5 minutes). Pour in fish stock; again cook until reduced by half (about 5 more minutes).

Pour tomato mixture into a food processor or blender; process until smoothly puréed. Transfer sauce to a bowl, season to taste with salt and pepper, and set aside. (At this point, you may cover and refrigerate for up to 24 hours.)

Pull beard from each mussel with a swift tug. Preheat a 13-inch paella pan or 5-quart sauté pan over medium-high heat until rim of pan is hot-to-the-touch. Add remaining 2 tablespoons (30 ml) oil and wait for about 1 more minute. Add garlic, 2 tablespoons of the parsley, and mussels. Increase heat to high, cover pan, and cook until mussels pop open (5 to 8 minutes). With a slotted spoon, transfer mussels to a bowl; keep warm. Discard any unopened mussels.

Add tomato sauce to liquid in pan and cook, stirring often, until reduced by about a fourth (3 to 5 minutes). Return mussels (and any liquid that has accumulated in bowl) to pan. Mix quickly to reheat mussels and coat them with sauce. Ladle mussels into warm shallow individual bowls. Sprinkle with remaining 1 tablespoon parsley.

Makes 8 servings

Prep: *About 30 minutes*
Cook: *30 to 35 minutes*

Per serving: *135 calories, 8 g total fat, 1 g saturated fat, 14 mg cholesterol, 240 mg sodium, 9 g carbohydrates, 2 g fiber, 7 g protein, 33 mg calcium, 3 mg iron*

This refreshing salad features an unusual dressing of puréed pineapple spiced with cayenne. Making the salad with packaged triple-washed spinach simplifies preparation.

Fresh Spinach Salad with Pineapple & Honey Dressing

French Bread Croutons (recipe follows) or ¼ cup (30 g) toasted pine nuts (see Cooking tips)

2 packages (about 6 oz./170 g each) fresh baby spinach, stems removed, leaves rinsed and crisped if necessary

2 cups (310 g) cubed fresh pineapple

⅓ cup (80 ml) honey

½ teaspoon salt

½ teaspoon ground red pepper (cayenne)

Prepare croutons and set aside. Place spinach in a very large bowl.

In a food processor or blender, combine pineapple, honey, salt, and red pepper. Process until smoothly puréed; add water, a few drops at a time, if consistency is too thick. (At this point, you may cover and refrigerate spinach and dressing separately for up to 4 hours.)

To serve, stir dressing and pour over spinach; mix gently. Sprinkle with croutons.

Makes 8 servings

French Bread Croutons. Cut day-old **French bread** into cubes to make about 2 cups (about 2 oz./55 g). Spread bread evenly on a cookie sheet. Bake in a 300°F (150°C) oven for 10 minutes. Meanwhile, preheat an 8- or 10-inch omelette pan over medium heat until rim of pan is hot-to-the-touch. Add 2 tablespoons (30 ml) **olive oil** and wait for about 1 more minute. Then remove pan from heat and stir in ¼ teaspoon **dried tarragon** and 1 small clove **garlic,** minced. Add toasted bread cubes to oil mixture and mix lightly until evenly coated. Spread on cookie sheet, return to oven, and continue to bake until crisp and lightly browned (20 to 25 more minutes). Let cool; then store in a covered container for up to a week.

Prep: About 15 minutes
Cook: 30 to 35 minutes

Per serving with croutons: 131 calories, 4 g total fat, 1 g saturated fat, 0 mg cholesterol, 236 mg sodium, 24 g carbohydrates, 2 g fiber, 2 g protein, 52 mg calcium, 2 mg iron

Cooking tips: If you like, use toasted pine nuts in this salad in place of the croutons. Place ¼ cup (30 g) pine nuts in an 8- or 10-inch omelette pan; stir occasionally over medium heat until golden (3 to 5 minutes). Then pour out of pan and set aside to cool.

Coated with a light, creamy sauce, this side-dish pasta is seasoned with garlic, two kinds of ham, and fresh basil.

Fettuccine Lucchese

1 pound (455 g) dried fettuccine

2 tablespoons (30 ml) olive oil

2 tablespoons (30 g) butter or margarine

¼ cup (45 g) finely diced onion

1 clove garlic, minced

3 ounces (85 g) thinly sliced prosciutto, cut into thin strips

3 ounces (85 g) sliced baked ham, cut into thin strips

2 tablespoons chopped fresh basil

½ cup (120 ml) evaporated skim milk or whipping cream

Freshly ground pepper

Fill an 8-quart stock pot three-fourths full of water; cover and bring to a boil over high heat. Then add pasta and cook, uncovered, just until al dente (8 to 10 minutes). Drain well and set aside.

Meanwhile, preheat a 4-quart chef's pan or 5-quart sauté pan over medium heat until rim of pan is hot-to-the-touch. Add oil and wait for about 1 more minute; then add butter and swirl pan until butter is melted. Add onion and garlic; cook, stirring often, for 2 minutes. Add prosciutto and ham; continue to cook, stirring often, until meats begin to look crisp (about 5 more minutes).

To prosciutto mixture, add basil and milk. Bring to a boil, stirring to loosen drippings from pan. Add pasta; mix lightly, lifting with 2 forks, until pasta is coated with prosciutto mixture. Season to taste with pepper.

Makes 8 servings

Prep: *About 10 minutes*
Cook: *About 25 minutes*

Per serving: 321 calories, 9 g total fat, 3 g saturated fat, 23 mg cholesterol, 376 mg sodium, 45 g carbohydrates,1 g fiber, 14 g protein, 62 mg calcium, 3 mg iron

Cooking tips: Evaporated skim milk is a low-fat alternative to whipping cream. Sauces made with it will be slightly thinner and less shiny than those made with cream. It's also a good choice for cutting fat calories when you make mashed potatoes or a creamy soup.

Refreshing orange flavor distinguishes this easy-to-cook chicken in a sweet-tart wine sauce.

Chicken Valencia

8 boneless, skinless chicken breast halves (about 3 lbs./ 1.35 kg total)

About ¹/₂ cup (60 g) all-purpose flour

2 to 3 tablespoons (30 to 45 ml) olive oil

1¹/₂ cups (360 ml) dry white wine

1 tablespoon (15 ml) lemon juice

1 tablespoon grated orange zest

¹/₃ cup (80 ml) orange marmalade

Salt and freshly ground pepper

Chopped Italian parsley

Orange slices

Rinse chicken and pat dry. Cut each piece into 2 thin slices as follows: place chicken on a cutting board, boned side down. Holding firmly in place under the palm of your hand, slice horizontally (as if butterflying, but cutting all the way through). Coat chicken lightly with flour on all sides; shake off excess.

Preheat a 5-quart sauté pan over medium heat until rim of pan is hot-to-the-touch. Add 2 tablespoons (30 ml) of the oil and wait for about 1 more minute. Add as many pieces of chicken to pan as will fit without crowding. Cook until lightly browned on bottom (3 to 5 minutes). Then turn over and continue to cook until meat in thickest part is no longer pink; cut to test (3 to 5 more minutes). As chicken pieces are cooked, place them on a warm platter and keep warm in a 200°F (95°C) oven. Add up to 1 tablespoon (15 ml) more oil to pan as needed.

When all chicken has been cooked, add wine and lemon juice to cooking pan. Increase heat to high and bring mixture to a boil, stirring to loosen drippings from pan. Cook, stirring often, until liquid is reduced by about half (3 to 5 minutes). Stir in orange zest and marmalade. Season to taste with salt and pepper. Pour sauce over chicken. Sprinkle with parsley and garnish with orange slices.

Makes 8 servings

Prep: About 10 minutes
Cook: 15 to 20 minutes

Per serving: *279 calories, 6 g total fat, 1 g saturated fat, 99 mg cholesterol, 121 mg sodium, 13 g carbohydrates, 0.1 g fiber, 40 g protein, 30 mg calcium, 2 mg iron*

Cooking tips: *When you sauté chicken or other meats, it's important not to crowd in more pieces than the pan can comfortably hold. Placing too much meat in the pan will cause it to steam in its own liquid—and you won't get the crusty coating you want.*

Flaming a dessert makes for a dramatic presentation—even when the dessert is as simple as this one. Any orange liqueur will give the sauce a pleasing flavor, but types with a higher percentage of alcohol, such as Cointreau or Grand Marnier, can be ignited more easily.

Peaches with Caramel & Black Pepper Sauce

8   *medium-size peaches (about 2½ lbs./1.15 kg total)*

¼   *cup (55 g) butter or margarine*

¼   *cup (55 g) firmly packed light brown sugar*

1   *teaspoon freshly ground pepper*

    About ¼ cup (60 ml) champagne or other brut or extra-dry sparkling wine

3   *tablespoons (45 ml) orange-flavored liqueur*

Peel, pit, and halve peaches. Set aside.

Preheat a 3-quart sauté pan over medium-high heat until rim of pan is hot-to-the-touch. Add butter and sugar; cook, stirring often, until mixture bubbles and begins to caramelize (about 3 minutes). Lightly mix in peaches, then sprinkle with pepper. Pour in champagne. Cook, stirring occasionally and turning peaches carefully, until peaches begin to soften (6 to 8 minutes); add more champagne, 1 tablespoon (15 ml) at a time, if needed to keep peach mixture moist.

Add liqueur; carefully ignite with a match (be sure pan is not beneath a vent, fan, or flammable items). Shake and swirl pan until flames are gone. Spoon into dessert dishes and serve at once.

Makes 8 servings

Prep: *About 20 minutes*
Cook: *About 15 minutes*

Per serving: *144 calories, 6 g total fat, 4 g saturated fat, 16 mg cholesterol, 62 mg sodium, 21 g carbohydrates, 2 g fiber, 1 g protein, 15 mg calcium, 0.3 mg iron*

Cooking tips: *Note: pepper for this recipe must be freshly ground; canned pepper will not work. If the pungent flavor of pepper doesn't appeal to you in a dessert, omit the pepper and replace it with ½ teaspoon freshly grated nutmeg.*

Breakfast with the Family

Why not treat the family to a splurge of a Sunday breakfast on a lazy weekend? This tempting array of morning classics doesn't take long to put together—you can assemble the fruit, omelettes, and potatoes while the fragrant muffins bake.

Minted Pineapple with
Melon & Lime

Spinach, Bacon & Gruyère Cheese
Omelettes

Balsamic Potatoes with Shallots

Blueberry Streusel Muffin Tops

Cinnamon-dusted Hot Chocolate
Coffee   Orange Juice

This recipe makes two generous cheese- and bacon-filled omelettes. Divide each in half for a total of four servings.

Spinach, Bacon & Gruyère Cheese Omelettes

6 *large eggs*

4 *teaspoons herbes de Provence;
or 1½ teaspoons dried thyme,
1 teaspoon dried basil,
1 teaspoon dried marjoram,
and ½ teaspoon dried
rosemary*

1 *tablespoon (15 ml) water*

2 *cups (110 g) lightly packed
chopped fresh spinach*

1 *tablespoon butter or
margarine*

4 *slices bacon (91 g total),
crisply cooked, drained, and
crumbled*

1 *cup (about 4 oz./115 g)
shredded Gruyère cheese*

In a large bowl, beat eggs, herbes de Provence, and water to blend well. Stir in spinach; then set mixture aside.

Preheat a 10-inch omelette pan over medium heat until rim of pan is hot-to-the-touch. Add half the butter; wait for a few seconds, or until butter melts, stops foaming, and takes on a golden color.

Spoon half the egg mixture evenly into pan and let cook for about 10 seconds. Then, as egg mixture begins to set, tilt pan and, using a fork, pull edge of omelette toward center of pan and let uncooked egg flow to edge; repeat, working around pan. Continue to cook, shaking pan as needed to prevent sticking, until omelette is cooked on bottom and moist on top (2 to 3 minutes). Sprinkle half the bacon and half the cheese over one side of omelette.

Use a spatula to fold omelette in half as you slide it out of pan onto a warm plate. Divide omelette in half; lift one half onto a second plate. Repeat to cook a second omelette, using remaining butter, egg mixture, bacon, and cheese.

Makes 2 omelettes (4 servings)

Prep: *About 15 minutes*
Cook: *5 to 8 minutes per omelette*

Per serving: *300 calories, 23 g total fat, 11 g saturated fat, 363 mg cholesterol, 342 mg sodium, 3 g carbohydrates, 1 g fiber, 21 g protein, 375 mg calcium, 3 mg iron*

Cooking tips: *To quickly clean a Calphalon Hard-Anodized pan between omelettes, sprinkle the pan with table salt and rub with a paper towel. The salt's abrasiveness will clean dry residue off the pan without cooling down the pan.*

Golden brown, fresh-cooked potatoes always make breakfast more of an occasion—and they're simple to prepare. This recipe features little red potatoes, cooked in their jackets and accented with a splash of balsamic vinegar.

Balsamic Potatoes with Shallots

1   *pound (455 g) small red thin-skinned potatoes (each 1½ to 2 inches/3.5 to 5 cm in diameter)*

2   *tablespoons (30 ml) olive oil*

3   *shallots (85 g total), thinly sliced*

2   *tablespoons (30 ml) balsamic vinegar*

¼   *cup (15 g) chopped Italian parsley*

   Salt and freshly ground pepper

Scrub potatoes and cut lengthwise into quarters; set aside. Preheat a 2-quart sauté pan or 10- or 12-inch omelette pan over medium heat until rim of pan is hot-to-the-touch. Add oil and wait for about 1 more minute. Reduce heat to medium-low; add potatoes and cook, turning and stirring often, for 15 minutes. Add shallots; continue to cook, stirring often, until potatoes are golden brown and tender when pierced (about 5 more minutes).

Drizzle potatoes with vinegar and continue to cook and stir for about 2 more minutes. Remove from heat and mix in parsley. Season to taste with salt and pepper.

Makes 4 servings

Prep: *About 10 minutes*
Cook: *About 25 minutes*

Per serving: *169 calories, 7 g total fat, 1 g saturated fat, 0 mg cholesterol, 13 mg sodium, 24 g carbohydrates, 2 g fiber, 3 g protein, 13 mg calcium, 1 mg iron*

Cooking tips: *The round red thin-skinned potatoes featured in this recipe are firm and waxy textured. They are also ideal for boiling and steaming, whether you're using them in potato salad or serving them "as is," drizzled with a simple parsley butter. Because they come to market directly from the field, they're often called "new potatoes."*

*For a refreshing fruit medley, combine 4 cups bite-size pieces of **fresh pineapple**, 2 cups mixed **cantaloupe** and **honeydew balls**, and 2 tablespoons slivered **fresh mint**. Squeeze on **lime juice** to taste. At the table, offer **honey** to add to taste.*

To many who love muffins, the best part is the crusty top—and now there's a muffin cap pan, specifically designed to bake "bottomless" muffins. Fresh from the oven, they're like big, thick, warm cookies, filled with juicy blueberries and crunchy with pecan streusel.

Blueberry Streusel Muffin Tops

2½ cups (310 g) all-purpose flour

1 cup (220 g) firmly packed brown sugar

½ cup (55 g) chopped pecans

2 teaspoons baking powder

1 teaspoon baking soda

½ teaspoon ground nutmeg

¾ cup (6 oz./170 g) cold butter or margarine, cut into pieces

1 large egg

⅔ cup (160 ml) low-fat or whole milk

1 cup (140 g) fresh blueberries (or unsweetened frozen blueberries, thawed)

In a large bowl, combine flour, sugar, pecans, baking powder, baking soda, and nutmeg; mix well. Using a pastry blender or 2 knives, cut in butter until mixture resembles coarse crumbs; set aside ¾ cup (about 100 g) of the mixture.

In a medium-size bowl, beat egg and milk until blended. Add egg mixture to flour mixture in large bowl, stirring just until dry ingredients are evenly moistened; stir in blueberries with last few strokes.

Spoon about ¼-cup (60-ml) portions of batter into all 12 indentations of 2 lightly greased muffin cap pans. Sprinkle evenly with reserved crumb mixture. Bake in a 350°F (175°C) oven until muffin tops are golden brown (about 20 minutes). Let muffin tops cool in pans on racks for about 5 minutes; then carefully remove from pans. Serve warm or at room temperature.

Makes 1 dozen muffin tops

Prep: *About 15 minutes, plus about 5 minutes to cool*
Cook: *About 20 minutes*

Per muffin top: *322 calories, 16 g total fat, 8 g saturated fat, 49 mg cholesterol, 324 mg sodium, 41 g carbohydrates, 1 g fiber, 4 g protein, 89 mg calcium, 2 mg iron*

Cooking tips: *You can make frothy hot chocolate in a Calphalon Professional Hard-Anodized 3½-quart water pitcher, bringing it directly from range top to breakfast table. Shake on a dusting of ground cinnamon before you pour the steaming chocolate into mugs.*

Brunch with Guests

*When friends or relatives
spend the weekend, treat
them to this leisurely
morning repast. Start with a
well-seasoned Bloody Mary
(with or without the vodka)
to sip as the oven pancake
and grits casserole are baking.*

Bloody Mary Cocktails

Dutch Baby with Papaya & Lime
Savory Turkey Patties
Baked Cheese & Garlic Grits

Coffee

The egg-rich batter that produces this pancake is easy to make in your food processor or blender. It puffs most dramatically when it's baked in a generously proportioned pan such as a paella pan.

Dutch Baby with Papaya & Lime

½ cup (4 oz./115 g) butter or
   margarine

6 large eggs

1½ cups (185 g) all-purpose
   flour

2 tablespoons granulated sugar

1½ cups (360 ml) milk

1 teaspoon vanilla

1 large papaya (about
   12 oz./340 g), peeled,
   seeded, and diced

Lime wedges

Powdered sugar

Place ¼ cup (55 g) of the butter in a 2- or 3-quart sauté pan, 10-inch everyday pan, or 13-inch paella pan. Place pan in oven as it preheats to 425°F (220°C).

Meanwhile, in a food processor or blender, combine eggs, flour, granulated sugar, milk, and vanilla. Process until smoothly blended.

When oven reaches 425°F (220°C), remove pan and swirl melted butter to coat inner surface evenly. Pour in half the batter. Return pan to oven and bake until pancake is golden brown and crisp around edges (20 to 25 minutes). Cut into wedges and serve immediately, with papaya, lime, and powdered sugar to add to taste.

Meanwhile, melt remaining ¼ cup (55 g) butter in pan. Then pour in remaining batter and bake second pancake.

Makes 2 pancakes (8 servings)

Prep: *About 10 minutes*
Cook: *20 to 25 minutes per pancake*

Per serving: *295 calories, 17 g total fat, 9 g saturated fat, 197 mg cholesterol, 188 mg sodium, 26 g carbohydrates, 1 g fiber, 9 g protein, 87 mg calcium, 2 mg iron*

Cooking tips: *You can identify a ripe papaya by its color: the skin should be more yellow than green. Most papayas are sold firm-ripe and need to be ripened further at home. To do this, enclose the fruit loosely in a paper bag and store at room temperature until the flesh feels about as soft as that of a ripe peach.*

Mild-tasting ground turkey is a good starting point for homemade breakfast sausage, since it offers such a gentle background for your favorite herbs and spices. These juicy patties are also enhanced by brandy-soaked dried cranberries.

Savory Turkey Patties

¼ cup (35 g) dried cranberries

2 tablespoons (30 ml) brandy

1 tablespoon butter or margarine

1 small onion (about 3 oz./ 85 g), finely chopped

1 clove garlic, minced

⅓ cup (15 g) soft bread crumbs

1½ teaspoons salt

1 teaspoon dried sage

1 teaspoon dried thyme

½ teaspoon ground nutmeg

½ teaspoon crushed red pepper flakes

¼ teaspoon white pepper

1 pound (455 g) ground turkey

1 pound (455 g) lean ground pork

2 teaspoons grated orange zest

¼ cup (15 g) chopped parsley

1 tablespoon (15 ml) vegetable oil

Fresh sage leaves (optional)

In a small bowl, combine cranberries and brandy; set aside for at least 10 minutes.

Meanwhile, preheat a 12- or 14-inch omelette pan over medium-high heat until rim of pan is hot-to-the-touch. Add butter and wait for about 1 more minute. Add onion and garlic; cook, stirring often, until onion is soft but not brown (2 to 3 minutes). Remove from heat.

In a large bowl, mix bread crumbs, salt, dried sage, thyme, nutmeg, red pepper flakes, and white pepper. Then lightly mix in turkey, pork, onion mixture, orange zest, parsley, and cranberry mixture. Shape turkey mixture into 16 patties, each about ½ inch (1 cm) thick.

Preheat pan in which onion was cooked over medium-high heat until rim of pan is hot-to-the-touch. Add oil and wait for about 1 more minute. Add patties in a single layer. Cook, turning once, until well browned on both sides (4 to 5 minutes per side). Lift out patties and place on a warm platter. Garnish with sage leaves, if desired.

Makes 8 servings

Prep: About 15 minutes
Cook: 10 to 15 minutes

Per serving: 281 calories, 18 g total fat, 6 g saturated fat, 78 mg cholesterol, 511 mg sodium, 5 g carbohydrates, 0.5 g fiber, 20 g protein, 33 mg calcium, 2 mg iron

In the South, grits are a standard part of the breakfast menu. If you're unfamiliar with grits, you might begin your acquaintance by sampling this well-seasoned casserole—after all, some say that grits could well be the polenta of the twenty-first century!

Baked Cheese & Garlic Grits

2   tablespoons (30 g) butter or
    margarine

1   small onion (about 3 oz./
    85 g), minced

2   cloves garlic, minced

¹/₃ cup (80 ml) milk

3   large eggs

1   teaspoon salt

4   cups (950 ml) warm cooked
    hominy grits

1   cup (about 4 oz./115 g)
    shredded Cheddar cheese

Preheat a 7-, 8-, or 10-inch omelette pan over medium-high heat until rim of pan is hot-to-the-touch. Add butter and wait for about 1 more minute. Add onion and garlic; cook, stirring often, until onion is soft but not brown (2 to 3 minutes). Remove pan from heat and set aside.

In a large bowl, beat milk and eggs until blended. Mix in salt, grits, cheese, and onion mixture. Spread mixture in a lightly greased 7- by 10-inch oval au gratin pan or other shallow 2- to 2¹/₂-quart casserole. Bake in a 350°F (175°C) oven until mixture is lightly browned on top and softly set in center (about 1 hour).

Makes 8 servings

Prep: *About 20 minutes*
Cook: *About 1 hour and 5 minutes*

Per serving: *194 calories, 10 g total fat, 6 g saturated fat, 104 mg cholesterol, 421 mg sodium, 18 g carbohydrates, 1 g fiber, 8 g protein, 129 mg calcium, 1 mg iron*

Cooking tips: *Follow the directions on a package of quick-cooking grits to prepare the 4 cups warm cooked grits.*

*To make **Bloody Mary Cocktails** for 8 servings, measure 8 cups (1.9 liters) **tomato juice.** Pour 2 cups (470 ml) of the juice into a blender; set remainder aside. To blender, add 5 tablespoons (75 ml) **Worcestershire sauce,** 1¹/₂ teaspoons **liquid hot pepper seasoning,** ¹/₂ teaspoon **dried basil,** ¹/₂ teaspoon **prepared horseradish,** ¹/₄ teaspoon **lemon pepper,** ¹/₄ teaspoon crushed **celery seeds,** and 1 teaspoon minced **parsley.** Process until well blended. Add this seasoned tomato juice to reserved plain tomato juice and stir well. (At this point, you may cover and refrigerate for up to 24 hours.)*

*To serve, rub rims of 8 glasses with a **lemon wedge;** dip rims in **seasoned salt** or coarse salt, then fill glasses with cracked **ice.** Squeeze a **lemon wedge** into each glass, then place wedge in glass; if desired, add 3 to 4 tablespoons (45 to 60 ml) **vodka** to each. Fill glasses with tomato juice mixture and stir well. Serve each cocktail with a **kosher dill pickle spear** as a stirrer; or hook a slit pickle slice over the rim of each glass.*

Basic Kitchen Equipment for Weekend Cooking

Whether you're equipping a kitchen in your first home or stocking your vacation getaway, these basic cookware and bakeware items are a must. With these fundamental pieces, you'll have everything you need to create many delicious dishes for all kinds of weekend meals, from candlelit dinner parties to breezy family picnics.

COOKWARE

8-, 10-, or 12-inch omelette pan: Doubles as a skillet.

2-, 3-, or 5-quart sauté pan: For braising for use as a covered casserole.

2- and 4-quart sauce pans: Add a **steamer insert** for versatility.

8-quart stock pot with pasta insert

5-quart saucier pan: Ideal for slow cooking on the range top or in the oven.

Large roasting pan with rack

PANS FOR BAKING

Medium or large cookie sheets (2): For everything from cookies to free-form loaves of bread.

8- or 9-inch-round cake pans (2 or 3)

8-inch-square pan

9- by 13-inch pan

4½- by 8½-inch or 5- by 10-inch loaf pans (2): For meat loaf, quick breads, and yeast breads.

12-cup muffin pan: Use it for cupcakes and yeast rolls, too.

OTHER KITCHEN ESSENTIALS

Without this basic equipment, your scope as a cook can be limited. Be sure your kitchen includes these.

    Colander
    Chef's knife
    Paring knife
    Slicing knife
    Serrated bread
      knife
    Sharpening
      steel
    Cutting board
    Mixing bowls
    Wire strainer
    Cooling racks
    Measuring cups
    Measuring spoons
    Kitchen scale

SPECIALTY ITEMS

Weekends give you the time to explore new culinary territory. When you're preparing ethnic dishes, a crowd-size casserole, or the catch of the day, consider using these specialty pans. Their varied sizes and shapes make them more versatile than their names suggest.

Stir fry pan: With a flat bottom and high, sloping sides, this 8- or 10-inch pan is a cross between a frying pan and a wok. Use it for both traditional Asian dishes and quick sautés.

Wok: Also useful for stir-fries is the traditional 14-inch wok. Its high, sloping sides make stirring and tossing easy; the steel ring can be used on both gas and electric ranges. Or choose the 12-inch flat-bottom wok, which can be placed directly on the heat source.

Fajita pan: This flat-bottomed, low-sided pan can be preheated in the oven, letting you bring fajita fillings to the table sizzling hot.

Paella pan: When you cook for a crowd, you'll appreciate this shallow pan with sloping sides, available in 13- and 16-inch sizes. Ideal for the traditional Spanish medley of rice and seafood, it's also perfect for sautéing meats and frying big batches of sliced bacon.

Fish poacher: Designed for poaching a whole fish, this 20-inch-long pan with a stainless steel insert can also be used for cooking fish steaks or thick fillets, poaching whole fruits, and steaming vegetables.

Covered casserole: Two loop handles distinguish this adaptable 3- or 4-quart round pan with a domed cover; it's attractive enough to come from the range or oven directly to the table. Use it for sautéing and braising, or as a soup or sauce pan.

Griddle: Choose the size that suit you best, whether it's a 13- by 20-inch rectangle, a 13- or 8-inch round, or an 11-inch square. These pans are perfect for making golden brown sandwiches and pancakes; the round griddles can also be used to bake pizza.

Grill pan: Available in both round (12-inch) or square (11-inch) shapes, this ridged range-top pan produces handsomely grilled steaks, chops, sausages, and chicken breasts in short order.

Pizza pan: Bake either a thick- or a thin-crusted pizza in this generous 14-inch-round pan. The dark surface browns and crisps the crust perfectly (be sure to remove the pizza to a cutting board before slicing it).

Angel food pan: A lofty angel food cake baked in this 10-inch-round tube pan is an irresistible low-fat dessert.

Crown BUNDT® pan: You'll use this graceful 10-inch pan for both luscious dessert cakes and buttery coffeecakes.

UTENSILS

The items on this list can make the difference between success and failure—and using them deftly will make you look like a pro.

- Mixing spoons (nylon, coated, or wooden if your cookware has a nonstick surface)
- Slotted spoon
- Vegetable peeler
- Whisks
- Spatulas (metal, nylon, and rubber)

- Tongs
- Zester
- Timer
- Citrus juicer
- Instant-read meat thermometer
- Grater
- Can opener (manual or electric)
- Rolling pin
- Wine opener
- Garlic press
- Brushes (for applying bastes and egg washes)
- Pepper mill

SMALL APPLIANCES

Even in a vacation home, you'll make frequent use of these multipurpose kitchen helpers.

- Electric mixer (if you bake a lot, both a heavy-duty mixer and a portable one)
- Blender
- Food processor
- Toaster oven

KITCHEN SAFETY

Be sure your kitchen is equipped with a **fire extinguisher** and that the adjacent area contains a properly installed **smoke detector.**

Stocking Up for Weekend Cooking

Always keep your kitchen well stocked: cooking and baking are more satisfying when you can depend on a good supply of the staple foods you use often. Here are some of the items that a resourceful pantry should contain.

Be sure to keep track of your pantry supplies so you can replenish them as needed when you shop for perishable foods.

When it comes to produce, let the season be your guide—visiting a farmer's market for spring asparagus or juicy summer strawberries or tomatoes can be the beginning of a wonderful weekend meal.

ON THE PANTRY SHELF
Many of these foods should be refrigerated after opening.

Canned tomatoes (diced, pear-shaped)
Tomato sauce and paste
Tuna
Canned and marinated artichoke
    hearts
Canned beans (black; red kidney; small white;
    pink or pinto)
Olives (whole and sliced ripe, calamata,
    pimento-stuffed green)
Roasted red peppers
Orange marmalade
Honey
Mild-flavored molasses
Light corn syrup
Peanut butter
Soy sauce
Worcestershire sauce
Liquid hot pepper seasoning
Canned chicken, beef, and vegetable broth; bottled clam
    juice
Solid vegetable shortening
Vegetable oil
Olive oil

Vinegar (distilled white, cider, red and white wine, balsamic, rice)
Rice (long-grain white; arborio or other short-grain white)
Grits
Couscous
Pasta (small shapes such as orzo; bite-size shapes such as
    rotelle or penne; strands such as spaghetti or fettuccine)
All-purpose flour and cake flour
Sugar (granulated, brown, powdered)
Salt
Baking powder
Baking soda
Vanilla and almond extracts
Cornstarch
Yellow cornmeal
Rolled oats
Dried fruits (seedless and golden raisins; currants, apricots,
    cranberries, cherries)
Semisweet chocolate chips
Unsweetened cocoa
Evaporated skim milk

IN THE LIQUOR CABINET
Dry red and white wine
Dry vermouth
Brandy
Bourbon
Orange-flavored liqueur

IN THE PRODUCE BIN
These don't need refrigeration, but they should be kept in a cool, dark, dry place. To guarantee freshness and flavor, buy vegetables more frequently and in fairly small quantities.

Garlic
Onions (yellow and red)
Shallots
Russet potatoes

IN THE REFRIGERATOR
Milk

Sour cream

Plain yogurt

Butter or margarine

Cheese (Parmesan, Cheddar, blue-veined, Swiss or Gruyère)

Eggs

Mayonnaise

Catsup

Dijon mustard

Salsa

Hoisin sauce

Dill pickles

Capers

Prepared horseradish

Lemons

Oranges

Salad greens

Carrots

Celery

Green onions

Parsley

Thin-skinned potatoes

Ginger root

Nuts (pine nuts, sliced almonds, pecans, walnuts)

IN THE FREEZER
Keep out-of-season fruits and vegetables in the freezer, so you'll have them when needed. Breads also keep best when frozen—unless you use them very quickly.

Ice cream or frozen yogurt

Raspberries

Blueberries

Cranberries

Orange juice concentrate

Tiny peas

Breads (firm-textured white, whole wheat, English muffins, bagels, pita)

Fine dry bread crumbs (plain and seasoned)

Tortillas (flour, corn)

ON THE SPICE AND HERB SHELVES
Allspice (ground and whole)

Basil (dried)

Bay leaves

Chili powder

Cinnamon (ground and sticks)

Cloves (ground and whole)

Crushed red pepper flakes

Cumin (ground)

Curry powder

Dill weed (dried)

Ginger (ground and crystallized)

Ground red pepper (cayenne)

Herbes de Provence

Marjoram

Mustard (dry and seeds)

Nutmeg (ground)

Oregano (dried)

Paprika

Pepper (ground white and black; whole black peppercorns)

Rosemary (dried)

Sage (dried)

Tarragon (dried)

Thyme (dried)

Index